Wh

of C ?

What is conceptual art? Is it really a kind of art in its own right? Is it clever – or too clever?

Of all the different art forms it is perhaps conceptual art which at once fascinates and infuriates the most. In this much-needed book Peter Goldie and Elisabeth Schellekens demystify conceptual art using the sharp tools of philosophy. They argue: that conceptual art is driven by ideas rather than the manipulation of paint and physical materials; that it challenges the very basis of what we can know about art, as well as our received ideas of beauty; and that conceptual art requires us to rethink concepts fundamental to art and aesthetics, such as artistic interpretation and appreciation.

Including helpful illustrations of the work of celebrated conceptual artists from Marcel Duchamp, Joseph Kosuth and Piero Manzoni to Dan Perjovschi and Martin Creed, *Who's Afraid of Conceptual Art?* is a superb starting point for anyone intrigued but perplexed by conceptual art – and by art in general. It will be particularly helpful to students of philosophy, art and visual studies seeking an introduction not only to conceptual art but fundamental topics in art and aesthetics.

Peter Goldie is Samuel Hall Chair in Philosophy at The University of Manchester; and has held posts at King's College London and Magdalen College, Oxford. He is the author of *The Emotions: A Philosophical Exploration* (2000) and *On Personality* (2004).

Elisabeth Schellekens is Senior Lecturer in the Philosophy Department at Durham University. With Peter Goldie she was a joint researcher in an AHRC Innovation Award project on philosophy and conceptual art. She is editor (with Peter Goldie) of *Philosophy and Conceptual Art* (2007) and author of *Aesthetics and Morality* (2007).

'*Who's Afraid of Conceptual Art?* is a philosophically substantive guide through the controversies and values of conceptual art executed with wit and intellectual verve. Accessible to all it is a must read for anyone interested in the nature and significance of conceptual art.' – *Matthew Kieran, University of Leeds, UK*

'Conceptual art has perplexed and provoked philosophers and art lovers for decades. Armed with perfectly chosen examples, clear and engaging arguments, and a genuine sympathy for their subject, Goldie and Schellekens explain why we are right to be perplexed and then show us how to appreciate the ingenuity and sheer craftiness of some of the most infamous and yet captivating specimens of recent art.' – *Dominic McIver Lopes, University of British Columbia, Canada*

'This very lively and stimulating book is the perfect cure for those who suffer from an uneasiness, or even a phobia, concerning conceptual art. Goldie and Schellekens do a wonderful job in making the philosophical issues accessible to readers lacking a specialized background, while also providing much to interest the more initiated reader. The treatment of conceptual art is well-informed, sympathetic yet critical, and liberally illustrated with engaging discussion of challenging examples.' – *David Davies, McGill University, Canada*

PETER GOLDIE AND
ELISABETH SCHELLEKENS

Who's Afraid of Conceptual Art?

Routledge
Taylor & Francis Group
LONDON AND NEW YORK

This edition published 2010 by Routledge
2 Park Square, Milton Park, Abingdon, Oxon OX14 4RN

Simultaneously published in the USA and Canada
by Routledge
270 Madison Ave, New York, NY 10016

Routledge is an imprint of the Taylor & Francis Group, an informa business

Typeset in Joanna MT and DIN by
Swales & Willis Ltd, Exeter, Devon
Printed and bound in Great Britain by
TJ International Ltd, Padstow, Cornwall

British Library Cataloguing in Publication Data
A catalogue record for this book is available from the British Library

Library of Congress Cataloging in Publication Data
Goldie, Peter.
Who's afraid of conceptual art? / Peter Goldie & Elisabeth Schellekens. — 1st ed.
p. cm.
Includes bibliographical references and index.
1. Conceptual art. 2. Art—Philosophy. 3. Aesthetics.
I. Schellekens, Elisabeth. II. Title.
N6494.C63G64 2009
709.04'075—dc22
2009019463

ISBN10: 0-415-42281-7 (hbk)
ISBN10: 0-415-42282-5 (pbk)
ISBN10: 0-203-86604-5 (ebk)

ISBN 13: 978-0-415-42281-9 (hbk)
ISBN 13: 978-0-415-42282-6 (pbk)
ISBN 13: 978-0-203-86604-7 (ebk)

List if illustrations

Preface

As the title suggests, this book is about conceptual art and about why so many of us feel fear, mistrust, and other negative emotions towards it. But more than this, it is about art in general, for it is only through drawing a contrast with traditional art that we can come to see what it is about conceptual art in particular that gives rise to these responses.

So this book is aimed at anyone who is interested in art and our responses to art. Much of what we say involves philosophical discussion, for we believe that philosophy is best placed to answer the kinds of questions that we address. But we do not require any prior philosophical knowledge on the part of the reader, although we hope that there will be plenty here to interest those who are already working in philosophy of art, including students and professionals. All that we require from the reader is intellectual curiosity about this most peculiar thing in our lives: art.

A word of advice to the reader, if we may. Some of the ideas in this book are quite complex, and it may take a little while to take them on board at a first reading. If you find you are stuck at a particular point, please do not give up, but read on, because we will very likely return to it later, and things will, we hope, become clearer as you progress.

We would like to acknowledge here the generous support of the Arts and Humanities Research Council for a research project at King's College London on conceptual art, during which the seeds of this book were sewn. We also would like to thank all those who attended the lectures and seminars that we gave on conceptual art at King's College London, and since then at The University of Manchester and Durham University. Many thanks too to Routledge's anonymous referees, and to all our other colleagues working in philosophy of art whose comments have proved invaluable to us – both specifically on the contents of this book, and, over the years, on all the many complex issues that conceptual art gets us thinking about. And finally, thanks to Tony Bruce and Adam Johnson of Routledge for their support and encouragement.

The Challenge of Conceptual Art

One

INTRODUCTION

The very thought that conceptual art is something that we could possibly be frightened of, as the title of this book suggests, might initially seem strange. Surely artworks are hardly going to leap out from their frames and attack you (although see Ad Reinhardt's *What do you represent?* (Figure 1.1), nor are they going to follow you home without your knowing about it (although see Vito Acconci's *Following Piece*, Figure 1.2). But a moment's reflection reveals that some kinds of art can, in fact, be genuinely threatening, and a threat is something that calls for at least a cautious approach. For conceptual art, rather like the products of many other kinds of ideas or intellectual processes, may well bring into question something that you believe in or are committed to. After all, the financier might quite rightly be afraid of Marxism, the Catholic Church of the writings of Martin Luther, or the literary conservative of the modernist writing of Virginia Woolf.

The last example is perhaps the most useful for our purposes. One reason why the reader of literature might be afraid of Virginia Woolf's *To the Lighthouse* is that it threatens some deeply entrenched views about what literature is and should be. In other words, the threat is not simply that the work is new (after all, the latest book by Tom Clancy is new, yet hardly a threat), but that it is radically different from what we are familiar with: different in a way that seems to imply that the 'received' ideas about what constitutes good literature have to be substantially revised or even rejected. In some cases,

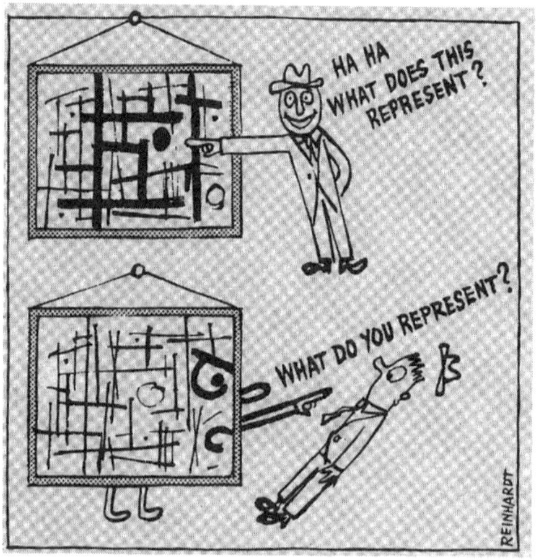

Figure 1.1 Ad Reinhardt, *What do you represent*?

(as provided by family)
ART COMIC by Ad Reinhardt
What Do You Represent
Courtesy Ad Reinhardt Foundation / Copyright Anna Reinhardt (provided by DACS)

then, we are afraid of art because it forces us to change our ideas so as to be able to make room for some different and unfamiliar aspect of our experience.

Of course there is another way of responding to this threat, namely by arguing that it isn't really a source of concern at all. According to this line of thought, one should stick by the canons (and the cannons) of the old ideas, and not feel obliged to accommodate new ones. One might, then, want to argue that the product of Virginia Woolf's pen isn't even literature to begin with *precisely because* it doesn't fit the traditional, familiar mould of what fiction is and should be. This approach need not be like that of the Ancien Régime in France before the revolution, of whom it was famously

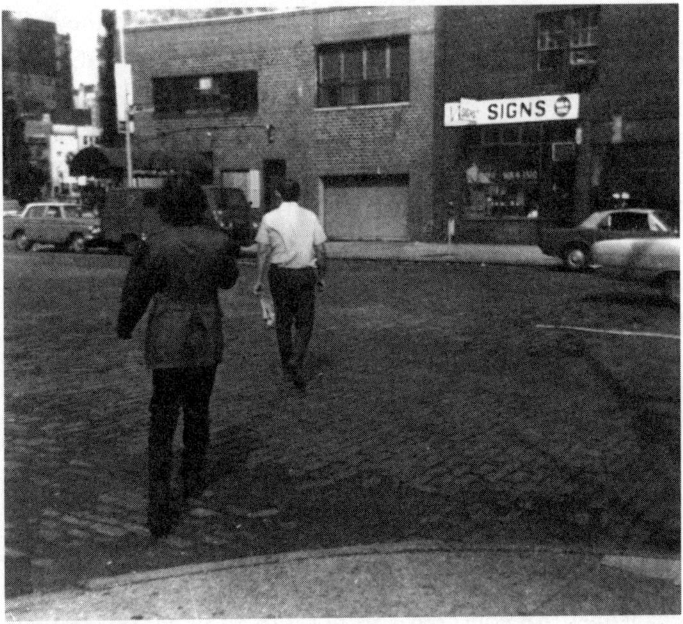

Figure 1.2 Vito Acconci, *Following Piece*.

Courtesy of Acconci Studio

remarked that they have forgotten nothing and learned nothing. Rather, the refusal to let in new ideas and revise one's old conceptions might be based on a proper and principled understanding of what art, for example, truly is.

It is important for our purposes that the mere fact that something is new is neither necessary nor sufficient for its being a threat to 'received' views in this way. After all, the Clancy example shows that newness on its own isn't sufficient for something to be a threat. What is more, Laurence Sterne's wonderfully zany *Tristram Shandy* (1759) reveals that newness is not a necessary condition to being a threat either. For one might feel equally threatened by this work – a work which was, as the Shandy character in the film based on the book (*Tristram Shandy: A Cock and Bull Story*, 2005) remarked, post-modern before modernism – as one might by Italo Calvino's *If on a Winter's Night a Traveller*, a paradigm of post-modern writing and published more than two centuries later. All that really counts for ideas to be threatening in the way we are interested in is that they be radically different from some more or less entrenched or received set of views. Either these views have to be revised or abandoned; or they have to be defended in the face of the onslaught from 'the different'.

How do these worries and concerns apply to the case of conceptual art? Before we can begin to see why one might be afraid of conceptual art in the sense just described, we must get a reasonable grip on what conceptual art is, for conceptual art is not the same as new or contemporary art. Once we have done that, we will be well placed to consider the many challenges that conceptual art poses to art in general and our conceptions of it. For there are several challenges that might explain why we often feel discomfort, doubt, fear, scepticism, aversion or even disgust in the presence of works of conceptual art.

Of course it is hardly the first time that innovative art has been considered profoundly challenging. Surrealism, Futurism and even Impressionism were all once thought of as deeply threatening. Let's take Impressionism for example, and remind ourselves of just how extreme some of the criticisms of it once were. Here is an extract from an article that appeared in *La Presse* on April 29, 1874:

> This school does away with two things: line, without which it is impossible to reproduce any form, animate or inanimate, and colour, which gives the form the appearance of reality.

Dirty three-quarters of a canvas with black and white, rub the rest with yellow, dot it with red and blue blobs at random, and you will have an *impression* of spring before which the initiates will swoon in ecstasy.

Smear a panel with grey, plonk some black and yellow lines across it, and the enlightened few, the visionaries, exclaim: Isn't that a perfect impression of the bois de Meudon?

When the human figure is involved, it is another matter entirely: the aim is not to render its form, its relief, its expression – it is enough to give an impression with no definite line, no colour, light or shadow; in the implementation of so extravagant a theory, artists fall into hopeless, grotesque confusion, happily without precedent in art, for it is quite simply the negation of the most elementary rules of drawing and painting. The scribblings of a child have a naivety, a sincerity which make one smile, but the excesses of this school sicken or disgust.

The famous Salon des Refusés, whose very name brings a smile to the lips – with its nut-brown women on yellow horses in forests of blue trees – that salon was a veritable Louvre in comparison with the Exhibition on the boulevard des Capucines.

In examining the works exhibited [. . .] one wonders whether one is seeing the fruit either of a process of mystification which is highly unsuitable for the public, or the result of mental derangement which one could not but regret. In this latter case, this exhibition would no longer be the concern of the critics, but of Dr. Blanche.

Despite the outrage provoked by new art movements such as Impressionism, most art is eventually absorbed into the fold of what we now think of as traditional art. Once we've come to understand what is being expressed in these new works, and the methods being used, we more often than not come to accept and even like them – as is the case, of course, with Impressionism. If conceptual art is different from other art movements in this respect, we'll need to find out why the challenges posed by this kind of art are radical in a manner that makes it resist assimilation into the history of (more or less) traditional art.

Some of these challenges, and our discussion of them, are quite complex and might not be completely transparent on a first reading. What we recommend, though, is to press on, for our approach in this book is to return to the same ideas on more than one occasion from different perspectives. The approach, in other words, is cumulative. But before we turn to the main task of this chapter, namely of asking what conceptual art is, there is one more preliminary thing to consider, the implications of which will resonate throughout the book. This is the question of the relation between conceptual art, common sense and philosophy.

CONCEPTUAL ART, COMMON SENSE AND PHILOSOPHY

Expressions such as 'traditional' or 'received' ideas might give the impression that the target of our investigation is merely the old-fashioned, died-in-the-wool thinking of a small minority who systematically refuse to move with the times, forgetting nothing and learning nothing. But this impression would be misleading. For what we're trying to get at are the ideas embedded in *our everyday common sense way of thinking* of art and of works of art. In other words, the traditional ideas about art that we have in mind here are the ideas that most of us share, whether we know it or not, and not just the ideas of the died-in-the-wool reactionary. This is what we mean by 'common sense'.

What, you may ask, has common sense to do with philosophy? Some readers might think that these two things have about as much to do with each other as fairness and the starvation of the poor. But this would be wrong. Common sense can play a very important role in philosophy, for it often serves as the starting-point of our examinations, a starting-point to which we apply *conceptual analysis*. Analysing the concepts that figure in our everyday common sense ideas about some notion or other enables us to gain a reflective understanding of that notion, and this is one of philosophy's main aims.

It might be helpful to illustrate this point by considering an example from outside literature and the arts, namely the notion of consciousness. This is as tricky a notion as you can imagine, and many philosophers and scientists despair of ever properly getting to grips with just what consciousness is. Nevertheless, consciousness is a notion of which we have a reasonable commonsense grasp, at least in what are sometimes called the 'central' cases. We can be quite sure, for example, that sticks and stones are not conscious and that you, reader, are conscious. However, when it comes to the more peripheral cases, our intuitions become less clear. For example, we might want to say that some animals such as cats and dogs are conscious but that others, such as jellyfish and lobsters, are not. Similarly, we might disagree about whether or not computers or robots ever could be conscious in any significant sense.

Let us dwell for a moment on this last question, whether or not things such as computers or robots could ever be conscious. To be interesting, it shouldn't be about any particular *existing* computer or robot; it should rather be about any *possible* such thing, of any degree of complexity. In short, you are being asked to think of a robot, as complex as you like – the robots of your favourite science fiction such as the Nexus 6 replicants in Ridley Scott's film *Blade Runner* (1982) – and then to consider whether it is *conceivable* that such a thing could be conscious. Obviously this isn't the place to discuss what the right answer to this question might be. The point, rather, is that this *kind* of question is meat and drink to conceptual analysis. First, we get a grasp of what we're talking about, in this case roughly what we mean by the term 'consciousness', through thinking about the central cases. Then we set up a *thought experiment* to test the concept in order to come to grips with our intuitions about whether or not the concept has any application in the context of the particular thought experiment at issue. This is an essential part of philosophy, and it shows that doing philosophy isn't just something done by professional academics and students: to ask whether a Nexus 6 replicant could be conscious is to ask a philosophically loaded question whoever is doing the asking.

Philosophical examination, through this process of conceptual analysis and using thought experiments, deepens our understanding of our commonsense notions, testing our intuitions about their application not only at the heart, but also at the boundaries, of the concept. It may well be that science will throw considerable light on what consciousness, say, really is, but we have to start with what *we* think – with our everyday commonsense notions – otherwise we won't even have a starting-point. As the British philosopher J. L. Austin said in another context:

> Certainly ordinary language has no claim to be the last word, if there is such a thing. It embodies, indeed, something

> better than the metaphysics of the Stone Age, namely . . . the inherited experience and acumen of many generations of men, [which] has been derived only from the sources available to ordinary men throughout most of civilised history: it has not been fed from the resources of the microscope and its successors [. . .] Certainly, then, ordinary language is *not* the last word: in principle it can everywhere be supplemented and improved upon and superseded. Only remember, it *is* the *first* word.[1]

What, you might ask, does all this have to do with conceptual art? Well, we have already seen that conceptual art challenges our traditional, commonsense, views about art. In this sense, one way of thinking of the challenges of much conceptual art, we will suggest, is in terms of what might be called *enacted thought experiments*. Analysing our everyday concepts about art is, then, not just about finding out what our ideas and views about art are. It is also about testing whether those ideas stand up to scrutiny, pushing the boundaries of our concept of what art is, what it should be, and how we can and should appreciate what is new and different. To see what we mean, and to see why the challenges from conceptual art are especially radical, let's now turn to a consideration of what conceptual art is.

WHAT IS CONCEPTUAL ART?

The trouble with trying to get a grip on conceptual art is that it's rather like trying to get a grip on a wet bar of soap in the shower: the more you try to tighten the grip, the more prone the soap is to slip out of your grasp. There is, in other words, something elusive about the very nature of conceptual art that seems to resist being summarised in one precise definition. It is even sometimes claimed that there are as many definitions of conceptual art as there are conceptual artists.

One approach to gaining an understanding of what conceptual art is would be to consider it in its historical context, as an art movement that took place at a certain time in a certain part of the world. Seen from this perspective, conceptual art – once referred to as 'modernism's nervous breakdown'[2] – is best grasped in relation to the movements that came before it and the sociopolitical background of the time. However, the problem that arises for this kind of historical narrative is that it runs the risk of paying too much attention to conceptual art's *particular* historical context, that is to say, roughly, the period between 1966 and 1972 and to the setting of New York, which we might think of as the period and place of high conceptual art (or what we'll capitalise as Conceptual Art).[3] This would involve the risk of missing out on much fascinating conceptual art that has been created outside that period, such as Marcel Duchamp's 'readymades' of the early 1910s, which encapsulate most or all of conceptual art's central characteristics, and which we will spend some time discussing. For perhaps, rather like *Tristram Shandy* which we described as post-modern before modernism, Duchamp's work can be described as conceptual before conceptualism. And perhaps there is also much conceptual art that has emerged since the time of high Conceptual Art. As the art critic Roberta Smith put it in her article 'Conceptual Art: Over and Yet Everywhere' in the *New York Times* of April 29, 1999: 'it's hard to think of a supposedly past art movement that feels more present . . . it is the shifting *terra infirma* on which nearly all contemporary art is built'. As we'll see, conceptual art does indeed go beyond the boundaries of the place and time of Conceptual Art.

Instead of the historical approach, the approach we will adopt will begin by considering some of the features or characteristics that are often taken to be associated with, or typical of, conceptual art, even if they are not definitive of it. As we progress, some of these characteristics will turn out to be more superficial than others, and getting to the heart of what conceptual art is, and what really makes conceptual art profoundly different from other kinds of art, will take us a considerable way past the end this chapter.

In spite of our earlier cautionary words about placing conceptual art in its historical context, let's begin with a bit of history, and with the most famous readymade of all, namely Duchamp's *Fountain* (Figure 1.3). The story is simple in its

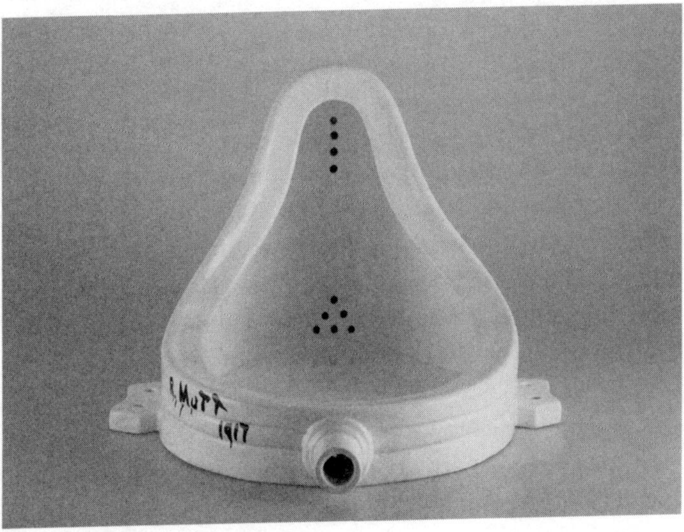

Figure 1.3 Marcel Duchamp, *Fountain*.

essential features.[4] In New York in 1916, the Society of Independent Artists, of which Duchamp himself was one of the Directors, put on an exhibition. The only criterion for entering an exhibit was that the artist had to pay an entry fee of six dollars. What Duchamp submitted as an entry, with the required fee, was a urinal that he had bought from a plumber's showroom. He had turned it upside down, titled it *Fountain*, and then signed it 'R. Mutt' (thus assuring anonymity) with the date 1917. The Directors of the exhibition, acting against their own criterion, refused it on the grounds that it was 'by no definition a work of art'.[5]

Fountain encapsulates many of the characteristics that are associated with conceptual art. Let's now see what these are. Remembering the bar of soap analogy, they won't be precise.

SELF-REFLECTIVENESS AND IRONY

As human beings, we are capable of having thoughts about our own thoughts, and feelings about our own feelings. For example, I might wish that I didn't want to eat big cakes, or I might feel ashamed of my anger. This self-reflectiveness is more than simply *awareness* of my thoughts and feelings, rather like you might be aware of the feeling of the carpet on your feet, for it involves some additional mental state over and above, and directed towards, the first mental state. This is quite an intricate mental activity, and it may be that other animals and very young children are not capable of it; dogs might be capable of shame and of anger but not capable of being ashamed *of* their anger, or being angry *at* their shame.

In a somewhat similar way, an artist, and derivatively a work of art, can be self-reflective, just as a comedian might make jokes about the difficulties he experiences in making jokes. Again, and as we have already seen, a novel might be reflective about what a novel is or should be, and about the activity and traditions of reading or writing a novel. This kind of self-reflectiveness is sometimes taken to be a mark of modernism, and is well exemplified by the novels of Virginia Woolf.[6]

Self-reflectiveness which is ironic goes one step further. It not only acknowledges its own activity, but also in some sense playfully pokes fun at it, teases it, or in some way undermines it. This ironic self-reflectiveness is exemplified by Duchamp's *Fountain*. Part of Duchamp's aim in his artistic statement was to challenge the definition of art and the role of the artist in art-making, and he did this in a highly self-reflective and playful manner. His work intentionally raises challenges such as these: 'How can something like a urinal be a work of art?', and 'How can the person who submitted this to an exhibition claim to be the "artist" when he has participated so little in its making?'. We might speculate that Duchamp would have been disappointed if the Society of Independent Artists had willingly accepted his entry to their exhibition. And we might also speculate that, in 1991, the British artist Gavin Turk would have been disappointed if his examiners at the Royal College of Art had accepted his submission for his final degree, consisting of a simple blue plaque of the kind seen all over London (such as 'Benjamin Disraeli, Earl of Beaconsfield, Prime Minister, lived in this house, 1872–1886'). Turk's plaque contained the words, 'Borough of Kensington: Gavin Turk, Sculptor, worked here 1989–1991'. Gratifyingly for him, it was rejected by his examiners, and then swiftly snapped up by the art market. Again what we see here is the ironic self-reflectiveness about art – and about art-making – that is characteristic of much conceptual art. Turk was making fun of his examiners, pointing towards how much they will disagree with the claim 'worked here' on the plaque, given that this is all he has to offer as evidence of his years of study.

Ironic self-reflectiveness, whilst characteristic of much of what we take to be conceptual art, isn't, however, going to be *definitive* of this kind of art. For some works that we take to be conceptual, such as Joseph Kosuth's *One and Three Chairs* (Figure 1.4), about which we'll have more to say later, don't have this feature. And other artworks that are ironically self-reflective are intuitively not conceptual. For example, Vermeer's *The Art of Painting* shows the artist in the picture painting the Muse of History, and yet, according to recent research, the work itself may well have been painted using the camera obscura; so in this painting Vermeer is arguably reflecting ironically on the art of painting.[7]

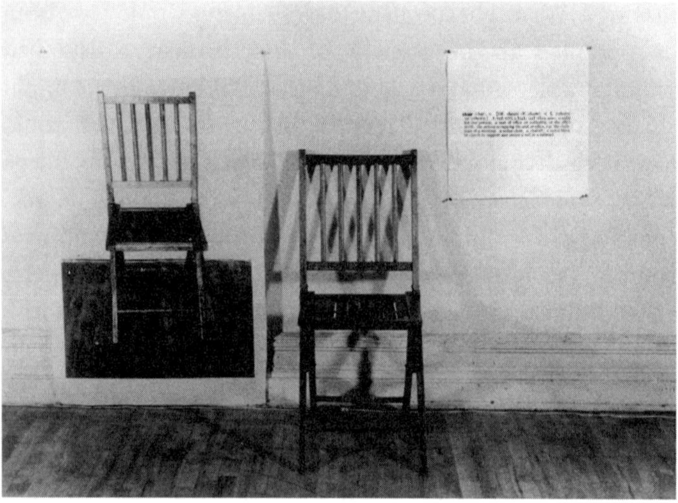

Figure 1.4 Joseph Kosuth, *One and Three Chairs*.

As we've seen, one manifestation of the self-reflectiveness of conceptual art lies in the way that it challenges our traditional ideas about what art is. In this sense, much conceptual art can be thought of as 'anti-definition', or against what people have traditionally taken to be the commonsense definition of art. Having said that, the worrying idea now begins to press in on us that perhaps anything *could be* art (which is not the same as the idea that everything *is* art), because all the artist has to do to create an artwork, it seems, is to submit it to an exhibition, or, even less, just to dub it art. Perhaps we will have to accept what the conceptual artist Donald Judd reputedly said: 'If someone calls it art, it's art'.[8]

The question of the definition of art will occupy us in Chapter two. However, we can already see one of the ways in which a conceptual artwork can be conceived as an enacted thought experiment, set up to challenge the accepted boundaries of the concept of art. Self-reflectiveness comes in again here. Something might arise that challenges the boundaries of a concept, but it could do so in a way that lacked this property of self-reflectiveness. For example, scientists might develop a method of cloning sheep that raises deep questions about the identity conditions of animals, but the scientists wouldn't be doing this *in order to* raise challenges to the concept of animal identity (at least let's hope that this would be no part of their intention). Or a heavenly body might be discovered whose existence challenges our concept of what a planet is. Similarly, perhaps, 'art' produced by a toddler, and early cave 'art', raise questions about whether such things really are art as we understand it. But raising these questions wasn't part of the aim of the toddler or the cave painter, and the questions aren't posed in the work itself in the self-reflective way we're interested in. In contrast, this goal was very much part of Duchamp's project when he submitted *Fountain* to the Society of Independent Artists. In another example (Figure 1.5), the wonderfully witty conceptual artist Piero Manzoni simply signed and dated a woman's arm. Was the arm now a work of art? And had Manzoni somehow sequestered the arm as *his* work through the gesture of signing it? Enacted thought experiments such as these raise, in a self-reflective and self-conscious way, challenges to our traditional notions of art and art-making.

One interesting implication that follows from the fact that much conceptual art has these two characteristics (ironic self-reflectiveness and anti-definition) is that it seems that to be a conceptual artist you must be *knowing* (in the meaning of the word when we talk of a 'knowing remark' or a 'knowing gesture'). For although there is a question of whether toddler 'art' or Neolithic cave 'art' really is art, one thing that a toddler and a Neolithic caveman couldn't be is a *conceptual* artist. For a toddler and a Neolithic caveman lack (we can safely assume) the required degree of self-reflectiveness about their practices of artmaking and about the art world that we would want to ascribe to a conceptual artist. As we'll see in many of the examples of conceptual art that we are going to examine in greater depth this sense of awareness and understanding will also involve knowing about *philosophy*, and about the relation between philosophy and conceptual art.

Again, though, this characteristic isn't going to be definitive of conceptual art. Whilst many works of conceptual art are anti-definition in the way we have been discussing, others, as we will see progressively in this book, are not concerned to challenge our ideas of what art is. So we must delve deeper to get to the heart of conceptual art.

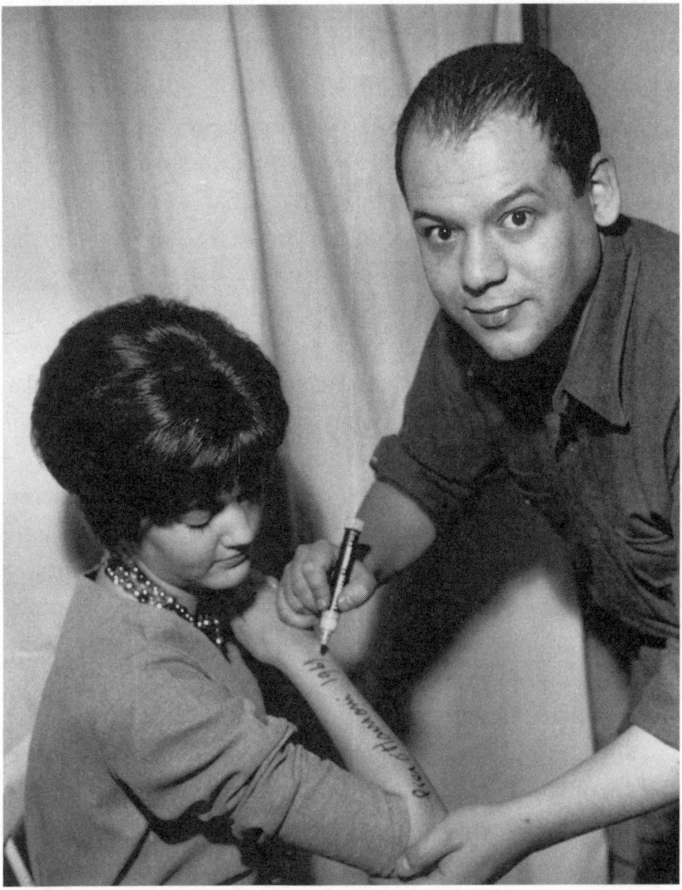

Figure 1.5 Piero Manzoni, Signed and dated a woman's arm.

Manzoni: © DACS 2009
Courtesy of Heart Herning Museum of Contemporary Art
Photographer Ole Bagger

AGAINST MEDIUM

The third characteristic of conceptual art that we want to consider is, like the second, a kind of self-reflective reaction against what has preceded it. Traditionally, art, as part of our commonsense thinking, has always been understood as being in a physical medium, with each particular art form employing a physical medium appropriate to it. So, for example, the art of painting is generally performed through working oils on canvases, acrylics on wood, and so on, with the 'and so on' limited in virtue of the art form being what it is. Similarly for sculpture and the other art forms: each one has its particular physical medium which is 'proper' to it. The term that we'll sometimes use to convey this idea is *medium-specificity*.

Let's consider painting in particular. A view considered characteristic of modernist painting was that flatness was one essential and unique feature of the medium of painting (whereas, clearly, this would not be a feature of the medium of sculpture or of architecture). This idea is found especially in the writings of the modernist critic Clement Greenberg. He considered flatness not to be a constraint on what painting can achieve, but a merit, something to be actively developed and finally taken to its limits. Here is a famous expression of this view by Greenberg in an essay of his called 'Modernist Painting':

> Realistic, naturalistic art has dissembled the medium, using art to conceal art. Modernism used art to call attention to art. The limitations that constitute the medium of painting – the flat surface, the shape of the support, the properties of the pigment – were treated by the old masters as negative factors that could be acknowledged only implicitly or indirectly. Under Modernism these same limitations came to be regarded as positive factors. . . It was the stressing of the

ineluctable flatness of the surface that remained . . . more fundamental than anything else to the processes by which pictorial art criticised and defined itself under Modernism. For flatness alone was unique and exclusive to pictorial art.[9]

Greenberg's idea, then, is that naturalistic art 'concealed' art by presenting us with an image of a scene – a landscape, for example – that would be very much like the image we would be presented with if we were actually looking at the landscape itself, and the role of the medium was simply to achieve that effect. In contrast, Greenberg says, in modernism, the medium (paint on canvas and so on) became not *just* a medium, but also essentially bound up with the aim of art: what became known as *medium-purity* was what art was itself *about*. The whole idea is brilliantly mocked in Tom Wolfe's wonderful book *The Painted Word*:

The business of flatness became quite an issue; an obsession, one might say. The question of what an artist could or could not do without violating the principle of Flatness – "the integrity of the picture plane," as it became known – inspired such subtle distinctions, such exquisitely miniaturized hypotheses, such stereotactic microelectrode needle-implant hostilities, such brilliant if ever-decreasing tighter-turning spirals of logic . . . that it compares admirably with the most famous of all questions that remain from the debates of the Scholastics: "How many angels can dance on the head of a pin?"[10]

So where can painting go from here? How can it escape from collapsing into the vortex of its tighter-turning spirals? Tom Wolfe has some very amusing things to say about this, and we will come back to them later. But the response of conceptual art was, in approach and in effect, radical. It was to reject not just flatness, but the whole idea of medium specificity and of the 'traditional' media of painting and of sculpture, in favour of new means of production that had not become so hidebound by the theorising of modernism. For example, in conceptual art we find such diverse – and for the time modernising – means of production as photography, video, events or 'happenings', installations, bodies, mixed media . . . and, like *Fountain*, readymades.

Once there was even a 'chew-in'. In 1966, John Latham, a part-time Lecturer at St Martin's College of Art in London, withdrew a copy of Greenberg's *Art and Culture* from the library. He then invited artists and students to the chew-in, at which they were each invited to tear out a page of the book, chew it, and spit out the remains into a receptacle. Latham then added chemicals to the pulp and eventually presented the end product to the School, titled *Still and Chew*, claiming to have 'distilled' *Art and Culture*. He is no longer at the St Martin's College of Art.

As we will soon see, the challenge of conceptual art to the traditional idea that art is in a physical medium has a wider scope than the kinds of diversity which we have just been considering. But even at this stage, the challenge is very significant to our commonsense way of thinking about art. It is, in the sense we discussed earlier, a *philosophical* challenge. In particular, conceptual art raises two challenges which we need to consider at this stage (more will come later): first, *ontological* (from the Greek word for 'being') or concerned with existence, and, second, *epistemological* (from the Greek word for 'knowledge') or concerned with knowledge.

The ontological challenge raises questions about what a conceptual artwork is, not in the sense of seeking a definition, but in the sense, roughly speaking, of where a conceptual artwork begins and ends. Gone are the easy times when art was to be found only in galleries and museums, and the physical bounds of a work were obvious for all to see.

The epistemological challenge is concerned with how we can *tell* whether something is an artwork or whether it is something else. When we study conceptual art, we see that it's no longer clear what is art and what is not. For example, one might wonder whether the pile of clothes in the corner of the room is part of the exhibition or just some workman's clothes put to one side for a moment, or whether the people marching with placards outside the White House are part of a political demonstration or a 'happening'. (A friend once asked a gallery curator where the exhibit was, and the curator replied 'You're in it, Sir'.)

An artwork that brings these two challenges together is Andy Warhol's *Brillo Boxes*. The Brillo boxes made by Warhol look just like those things that you could find in the supermarket – they are (virtually) perceptually indistinguishable – they are *indiscernible* (to use the term we will adopt in Chapter two).[11] Nevertheless, Warhol's boxes are art, while the others are not. What Warhol's work has achieved is what the contemporary philosopher Arthur Danto called, in his book of this name, *the transfiguration of the commonplace*: the commonplace, in this case the Brillo boxes, have been transfigured into art, *Brillo Boxes*.[12] The ontological challenge, on the one hand, is concerned with what it is that makes *Brillo Boxes* art and the Brillo boxes not art, and how the commonplace can be transfigured into art. The epistemological question, on the other hand, is about how we can tell that one is art and the other isn't, given that they are indiscernible.

DEMATERIALISATION OF THE ARTWORK

Let's turn now to an even more profound and radical challenge which conceptual art raises concerning the medium of art, and which will get us closer to the heart of what conceptual art is. This is a challenge to the very idea that an artwork has to be in a physical medium at all. As Lucy Lippard saw, conceptual art fundamentally 'dematerialises' the art object in so far as the artwork is no longer to be thought of as the material object that we can touch, see and feel in a gallery or museum.[13]

To help us grasp what dematerialisation really involves, let's consider a 'piece' (in some ways a less misleading term than 'work' which seems something of a practical contradiction as we will see later) which dates from the period of high conceptual art, or Conceptual Art. It is Vito Acconci's *Following Piece* (Figure 1.2), which is described thus: 'Activity, 23 days, varying durations. Choosing a person at random, in the street, any location, each day. Following him wherever he goes, however long or far he travels. (The activity ends when he enters a private place – his home, office, etc.)'.

The central questions here are these. What – and where – is the artwork in this case? (These are ontological questions.) Moreover, how can we tell what the 'artwork' is, and how can we gain access to it in order to appreciate it? The event described in *Following Piece* took place in 1969. It is therefore long gone, and the only access that we have to it is documentation in the form of some not very good photographs – and surely *these* aren't what we are supposed to focus on in artistic appreciation; they are in fact staged photos taken after the event took place. (These are epistemological questions.) On the whole, traditional artworks can readily be individuated and accessed for appreciation by going to the gallery or to the public place where the works are 'exhibited'. But with *Following Piece* not only do we not have an exhibition, we don't even have a physical *object* at all – there is no art work as such. Or at least so it seems.

Dematerialisation gets us closer to the heart of conceptual art. And this is so even though not all works of conceptual art completely lack a physical 'presence'. This must initially appear confusing, and it won't be until Chapter three that it will become clearer. But a few words here might be helpful to set the scene for later.

In a traditional work of art – an oil painting let's say – the painting's content (roughly speaking what it is about), and what it expresses, are appreciated *through* our appreciation of the physical medium: the oils on the canvas and the way that the oils have been worked by the artist. Moreover, this medium which we focus on is essential to our appreciation of the artwork. This is why the artist's skill matters so much in traditional art.

With conceptual art, even where there are physical objects present, or where there is a performance as in *Following Piece*, the skill of the artist doesn't seem to have the same kind of importance: the quality of the performance or of the photographs in *Following Piece*, for example, isn't a concern to us in at all the same way as the quality of the performance by the ballet dancer Agnes Oaks, or the quality of the photographs in the work of Bill Brandt.

One might just say dismissively that the conceptual artist is simply lazy or incompetent, or can't be bothered to learn the necessary skills and to take the time that artists and performers do in the traditional arts. But this, we think, is the wrong response. There is, we think, a *reason* why the physical material and the performance matter less. The reason is to be found in a distinction which we will come to in Chapter two and Chapter three. This is the distinction between *medium* and *means*: what in traditional art would be the medium (the oils on the canvas worked by the artist) in conceptual art is *merely* the physical means; accordingly, it is not essential to our appreciation of the work in at all the same way. In conceptual art, the medium is the *idea*. This remark, bound to seem gnomic at this stage, will, we hope, become clearer as we progress. But it should already be apparent that conceptual art is anti-medium not in the sense of insisting that there is no medium at all by which the artist communicates his or her artistic statement; it is, rather, that conceptual art insists that there is no physical medium.

So conceptual art differs from traditional art in two ways here. First, it draws on a wide variety of means of production of artworks. And second, these means of production are *mere* means. They are not the artistic medium, and consequently, as we will see, they are not the proper objects of aesthetic appreciation.

These questions of definition, of ontology, and of epistemology aren't merely abstract questions for philosophers. They have very important implications for how, what and why we go about appreciating conceptual art, as compared with traditional art. For whereas with traditional art we know what to look out for, conceptual art gives us a whole new set of criteria by which to appreciate and assess art. This brings us to another of conceptual art's challenges – its challenge to the traditional idea of the aesthetic.

AGAINST THE AESTHETIC

Try to remember a recent occasion when you were in an art gallery, and found yourself particularly and very favourably struck by one of the works on display – a picture in the Western European tradition, say, from the eighteenth or nineteenth century. Now try to remember what your experience was like whilst you were looking at the picture. Pleasurable or delightful, perhaps, but a special kind of pleasure or delight, one which is directed towards, and derived from, certain features of the picture – its elegance, for example, or its harmony, or the subtle way in which the artist has captured the play of light on the pearl earrings worn by the girl portrayed in the picture. This activity of grasping, through perception, these kinds of features and properties and of undergoing this kind of experience is part of what we call the *aesthetic*.[14]

Even with only this rough idea of the aesthetic in place, *whatever* the answers might be to the definitional, ontological and epistemological questions that we have been considering so far, it seems that, in works of conceptual art such as *Following Piece*, there *is* no suitable physical object or performance which might even *aspire* to give rise to this sort of feeling. (As we have discussed, it is surely not the photographs, which are mere *documentation*; and the action, the 'performance' is in the past and cannot be perceived in the required way.) So the traditional idea of the aesthetic, as involving a perceptual encounter with a physical object's or performance's perceptible aesthetic properties seems to be in difficulty. And this leads us to question what it is we are looking for and what we aspire to when we experience art.

Yet again, Duchamp seems to have set the agenda for conceptual art. Admittedly, with *Fountain* we do have a physical object, and admittedly the urinal does have a rather sleek and shiny appearance that can be pleasurable to look at. But to think that the urinal itself is an object intended to be contemplated for its *aesthetic* properties, specifically for its beauty, and that Duchamp was in effect trying to reveal to us this beauty, otherwise hidden from us in its very everydayness (for men at least), would be a serious mistake.

To back this up, let's see what Duchamp himself writes on the subject, about another of his readymades:

> In New York in 1915, I bought at a hardware store a snow shovel on which I wrote 'In advance of a broken arm'. It was around that time that the word 'Readymade' came to mind to designate this form of manifestation. A point which I want very much to establish is that the choice of these 'Readymades' was never dictated by an aesthetic delectation. This choice was based on a reaction of *visual* indifference with at the same time a total absence of good or bad taste . . . In fact a complete anaesthesia. One important characteristic was the short sentence which I occasionally inscribed on the 'readymade'. That sentence instead of describing the object like a title was meant to carry the mind of the spectator towards other regions more verbal'.[15]

This apparent rejection of the traditional notion of the aesthetic, found in different ways in *Following Piece*, in the pile of clothes in the corner, and in Duchamp's readymades, will be a major concern of the rest of this book. What do we expect in our experiences of art? Does conceptual art's rejection of the aesthetic explain our adverse responses to it as art? How is the rejection of the aesthetic connected with our contrast between physical medium and mere means? And what can conceptual art offer us if it doesn't offer aesthetic pleasure? Or perhaps conceptual art doesn't *really* reject the aesthetic altogether; perhaps it's only 'anti' the *traditional* notion of the aesthetic? We must wait and see.

FROM WORDS TO THE IDEA IDEA

It seems almost banal to point out that traditional art – pictures and sculptures in particular – centres on *illustrative* representations. It reserves *words* for the title, which would typically convey what the picture, for example, is a picture of. A picture of a person in robes and ermine, holding a sceptre and orb, might be titled 'George IV' so that the viewer can appreciate that it is George IV who is depicted.

But conceptual art is different. Consider in contrast to the picture of George IV a work by Joseph Kosuth of 1966, '(Titled Art as Idea as Idea), [Water]' Figure 1.6. Here we have a simple negative photostat of a dictionary definition of the word 'water'. Again, surely the mere photostat is not the work of art, but just its 'documentation' (not medium but means). Kosuth himself is on record as saying 'I never wanted anyone to think that I was presenting a photostat as a work of art'.[16] So here not only do we have the definitional, ontological, epistemological and aesthetic challenges of much the same

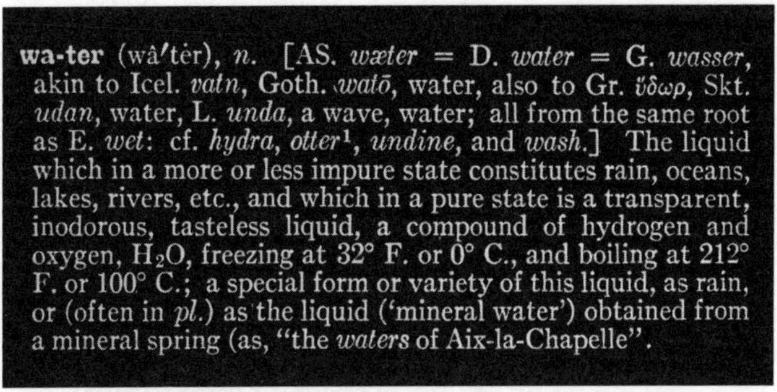
wa-ter (wâ′tėr), *n.* [AS. *wæter* = D. *water* = G. *wasser*, akin to Icel. *vatn*, Goth. *watō*, water, also to Gr. *ὕδωρ*, Skt. *udan*, water, L. *unda*, a wave, water; all from the same root as E. *wet*: cf. *hydra*, *otter*¹, *undine*, and *wash*.] The liquid which in a more or less impure state constitutes rain, oceans, lakes, rivers, etc., and which in a pure state is a transparent, inodorous, tasteless liquid, a compound of hydrogen and oxygen, H_2O, freezing at 32° F. or 0° C., and boiling at 212° F. or 100° C.; a special form or variety of this liquid, as rain, or (often in *pl.*) as the liquid ('mineral water') obtained from a mineral spring (as, "the *waters* of Aix-la-Chapelle".

Figure 1.6 Joseph Kosuth, (*Titled Art as Idea as Idea*), *[Water]*

Solomon R. Guggenheim Museum © 2007 Joseph Kosuth/Artists Rights Society (ARS), New York
Kosuth: © ARS, NY and DACS, London 2009.

kind as works like *Following Piece* raise. We also have this phenomenon of *words* being at the heart of the work – reminding us of Duchamp's comment on his work which we have just seen, about his aim 'to carry the mind of the spectator towards other regions more verbal'.

Let's consider now Rosemarie Trockel's *Cogito Ergo Sum* (Figure 1.7). The Latin words in front of us as we look at the piece 'I am thinking, therefore I exist' are the words used by Descartes as an expression of a kind of self-guarantee of his own existence. His very act of thinking 'cogito' or 'I am

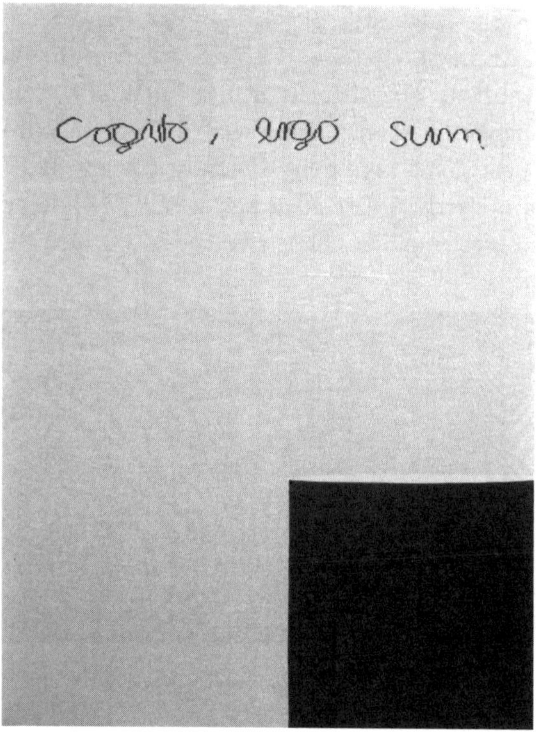

Figure 1.7 Rosemarie Trockel, *Cogito Ergo Sum*.

thinking' and thus being able verbally to express those words, enabled him, he believed, to reach the conclusion that he could know that he existed (ergo sum). What is curious about this Trockel piece is that it is made of wool and the words are knitted into the wool. But more curious still is the fact that the words are *machine* knitted. This is a rather nice philosophical joke: of course, the knitting machine's producing the words 'cogito' doesn't in any way show that the machine *thinks*, or that it can reach the conclusion that it exists, any more than would your computer have been shown to think if you programmed it to come up with the words 'cogito ergo sum' every time you turned it on.[17]

There is another issue that Trockel's piece brings to the fore: the fact that the words were machine-knitted is not evident from the piece itself; for all we know, the words might have been hand-knitted. So her *Cogito Ergo Sum* depends on language not only in the sense that it contains words as part of the work. It also depends on language in the sense that knowledge of facts, such as the fact that it was machine-knitted, is essential for appreciation of the piece – you wouldn't get the philosophical joke otherwise. We will call these facts *background discourse*. Now, when knowledge of background discourse like this – background knowledge – is essential for appreciation of the piece, we will say that appreciation of this work is *discourse dependent*.

Furthermore, the background discourse of Trockel's piece is what we will call *esoteric*, in the sense that the required background knowledge isn't available to a generally well-informed viewer from direct experience of the work, or even from the title of the work, which says nothing about its having been machine knitted. This might seem to present a real problem in the appreciation of conceptual art when compared with traditional art – the expectation of esoteric background knowledge seems somehow *unreasonable* or *unfair*. After all, one doesn't need any esoteric background knowledge to appreciate a Canova sculpture of a naked woman. All one needs is the physical object and a bit of knowledge about the contours of the human body. We'll see in Chapter five whether this really is something special about conceptual art as compared to traditional art, and whether it really is such a hamper to its proper appreciation.

Conceptual art's background discourse is sometimes esoteric in another way – in the sense of being about the artist, or *autobiographical*. Of course, there is nothing esoteric about autobiographies as such, nor is there any problem with an artist's revealing something about herself in her work, in the way that, for example, Jane Austen reveals her ironic stance towards society in her novels. The issue here is different though, and in Chapter five we'll also be discussing whether this esotericism is part of the explanation of why so many people feel frustration and resentment at conceptual art: 'The art world talking to the art world', as some would have it.[18] To put it bluntly, we might feel left out.

There is yet one more point concerning conceptual art's being discourse-dependent that we would like to raise here, for this too could be a source of frustration and resentment, namely the philosophical ambitions of conceptual art. These ambitions, as we'll see, will turn out to be highly relevant not only because philosophy will help us better to understand why our commonsense views about art seem to be threatened by conceptual art. They will also be highly relevant because philosophy will help us better to understand the *content* of many particular pieces, where the intentions behind the piece are in some way philosophical.

Trockel's *Cogito* is one such piece – it is philosophically *knowing* and it requires philosophical background knowledge in the sense we've just been discussing. But there is also another piece that we want to mention, especially since it will come up again a number of times as we proceed in our examination. The piece is Joseph Kosuth's *One and Three Chairs* (Figure 1.4). The intentions behind this piece are principally philosophical, pointing towards a discussion in metaphysics as old as Plato's, namely the relation between the three 'things' in the work: an ordinary chair, a photograph of a chair, and a dictionary definition of 'chair'. Is the 'real' chair still a chair as such, now that it is part of an artwork? Is the 'real' chair (if that is what it still is) more 'real' than the photograph of the chair, when both are equally part of the artwork? And what about the dictionary definition of 'chair': is that 'real' – eternal perhaps – in a way than neither the chair nor the photograph is? Kosuth is *saying something* to us, something philosophical, and he is doing so in a way that is quite different from the way that, for example, one of Chardin's still lives says something to us. (And, again, note the self-conscious lack of artistry or skill; the photograph wasn't even taken by Kosuth.) To cite Kosuth himself, 'The very stuff of art is indeed greatly related to "creating" propositions'.[19]

So it seems that the relationship that conceptual art has with philosophy is special. In the words of Arthur Danto in his *The Transfiguration of the Commonplace*:

> Art [has] itself evolved in such a way that the philosophical question of its status has almost become the very essence of art itself, so that the philosophy of art, instead of standing outside the subject and addressing it from an alien and external perspective, became instead the articulation of the

> internal energies of the subject. It would today require a special kind of effort at times to distinguish art from its own philosophy . . . so that little if anything is left over for the pleasure of artlovers. . . . Art has re-enacted [a Hegelian] speculative course of history in the respect that it has turned into self-consciousness, the consciousness of art *being* art in a reflexive way that bears comparison with philosophy, which itself is consciousness of philosophy.[20]

Danto's remarks suggest that conceptual art and philosophy are now more or less in the same business – and indeed many conceptual artists believe that to be the case. The whole emphasis on words, on the theory of art, on philosophy, either found in the work itself, or in some essential background discourse, is really the central target of Tom Wolfe's book, as evidenced by the title, *The Painted Word*. Returning to the metaphor he used in the citation above, Wolfe ends his book thus, nicely summing up what many people think is so threatening about our chosen characteristics of conceptual art:

> So it was that in April of 1970 an artist named Lawrence Weiner typed up a work of art that appeared in *Arts Magazine* – as a work of art – with no visual experience before or after whatsoever, and to wit:
>
> 1. The artist may construct the piece
> 2. The piece may be fabricated
> 3. The piece may not be built
>
> Each being equal and consistent with the intent of the artist the decision as to condition rests with the receiver upon the occasion of receivership.

Wolfe comments thus on this piece:

> And there, at last, it was! No more realism, no more representational objects, no more lines, colors, forms, and contours, no more pigments, no more brushstrokes, no more evocations, no more frames, walls, galleries, museums, no more gnawing at the tortured face of the god Flatness, [. . .] and in that moment of absolutely dispassionate abdication, of insouciant withering away, Art made its final flight, climbed higher and higher in an ever-decreasing tighter-turning spiral until, with one last erg of freedom, one last dendrytic synapse, it disappeared up its own fundamental aperture . . . and came out the other side as Art Theory! ... Art Theory pure and simple, words on a page, literature undefiled by vision, flat, flatter, Flattest, a vision invisible, even ineffable, as ineffable as the Angels and the Universal Souls.[21]

WHERE WE'VE BEEN AND WHERE WE'RE GOING

With roots as far back as Duchamp and branches reaching out to what is still being produced today, we've seen that conceptual art has certain characteristics that are typical of it: anti-definition, anti-medium, de-materialised, anti-aesthetic, linguistic, esoteric, ironic, and self-reflective.

But we think that what is at the heart of conceptual art, and what many of these characteristics point towards, is what we will call the *idea idea*. In traditional art such as painting, the medium for expressing the artist's vision – his or her artistic statement – is the physical medium: the oils on the canvas which have been worked in a special way. In conceptual art, *there is no physical medium: the medium is the idea*. This is, in essence, the 'idea idea'. In what is to come in the rest of this book we hope to make sense of the idea idea, to show in what ways it is definitive of what conceptual art is, and why understanding the idea idea matters so much in our appreciation of conceptual art. As the American conceptual artist Sol LeWitt put it in the opening sentences of his famous 'Paragraphs on conceptual art' in *Artforum* 1967, '[i]n conceptual art the idea or the concept is the most important aspect of the work. When an artist uses a conceptual form in art, it means that all of the planning and decisions are made beforehand and the execution is a perfunctory affair'.[22]

Aren't we right, then, to feel that our traditional commonsense notions of art are being threatened, and to feel resentment and frustration at what the art world is putting in front of us for our appreciation? Or are our everyday commonsense ideas about what art is, and what art ought to be, really so inviolable that we should dismiss all conceptual art outright, as failing to match up to what we expect? Perhaps what we've called the enacted thought experiments of conceptual art really *ought* to make us rethink some of our traditional ideas about art and about the aesthetic. Then perhaps we would be better able to understand and appreciate conceptual art for what it is, rather than constantly holding it up for comparison (unfavourable comparison) with traditional art. Perhaps this will help us to sort out what's good conceptual art from what's not so good with more confidence than we have in the past. And perhaps doing some philosophy will help us in facing up to these challenges. We shall see.

The Definition and the Thing
Two

INTRODUCTION

In the last chapter we got a rough grasp of what we mean by conceptual art, at the heart of which, we suggested, is the *idea idea*. However, we were also left with a considerable amount of outstanding business: a plethora of questions and challenges that we need to examine if we are to understand conceptual art better. In particular, we are yet to address the issue of what we mean by 'art'. When we have tackled that concern, we can return to another set of questions that we touched on briefly in Chapter one but didn't explore in any detail, namely questions of ontology. This, you will recall, concerns what kind of thing an artwork is. Only once we have answers to these questions will we be in a position in Chapter three to consider the epistemology of conceptual art (questions to do with knowledge) and to form an assessment of particular pieces of conceptual art, be it of praise or condemnation. This method is in itself a controversial one, and we'll need to support it as we proceed.

Sometimes, of course, questions of this kind don't matter so much: in some spheres of activity we can just get on without worrying about the subtleties. For example, if you are with a group of friends, drinking and eating together in a convivial atmosphere, and someone asks whether your gathering meets the definition of a *party* or whether it is merely a gathering, and whether the party's boundaries extend into the corridor outside the apartment, or whether they are restricted to the space owned by the host, it would be with good reason that you gave a shrug and just got on with the fun. For in this case the questions of definition, ontology and so on don't impinge on proper appreciation of the evening's events. Art, we are claiming, is different in this way: appreciation depends on definition, ontology and epistemology, and this is especially so with conceptual art.

Yet, you might protest, surely we manage to appreciate art perfectly well – eighteenth- and nineteenth-century paintings in London's National Gallery or New York's Metropolitan Museum of Art for example – without having settled these questions in advance. If we manage all right here, why might we not succeed equally well when we turn to conceptual art? Our reply to this protest is that our encounters with traditional art can only be described in this way because we tacitly *presuppose* certain answers to our questions.[23] We might not always be aware of exactly what those answers are, or of what follows from them, but nevertheless they ground our experience of traditional art. With conceptual art, in contrast, we find ourselves adrift in uncharted waters. The questions rise to the surface like worrying outcrops of rock, and the answers don't readily come to us.

To see how our presuppositions work in our engagements with traditional art, let's pause to consider an example such as Botticelli's *Birth of Venus*. Here, we presuppose a definition. That is to say, we presuppose that *whatever* the definition of art turns out to be, this picture had jolly well better be art, and anyone who comes up with a definition suggesting otherwise is *obviously* wrong. We think of it as a paradigm case of art. What is more, we presuppose the ontology. In other words, we presuppose that the object that is the work of art is the picture itself, the marks and brush-strokes on the canvas. Just think about how we would respond if someone said that we should also include the piece of wire on which the picture is hanging in the proper object of appreciation. We would respond by saying that the wire *obviously* isn't part of the artwork. Finally, we presuppose the epistemology. We take for granted that the proper way to gain access to the work in order to appreciate it properly is by looking at it from front on, in good lighting conditions, and so on. The suggestion, for example, that an adequate appreciation of *Birth of Venus* could be gained by reading about it in a textbook, inspecting a postcard reproduction of it, or by looking at it from side-on, horizontal to the canvas, is *obviously* wrong, and anyone who suggested otherwise would meet with deserved ridicule.

So, with traditional art, it isn't as though the questions we have raised so far don't matter (as they don't when it comes to the case of the party or gathering). In fact, they matter very much, as is evidenced by our response to the person who suggested that *Birth of Venus* wasn't art, or the person who started to admire the piece of wire holding up the picture, or the person who thought that it is sufficient for appreciation of the work to read about it in a textbook. It's just that with traditional art we think the answers are obvious. Obviously, the *Birth of Venus* is an artwork; obviously the wire isn't part of the work; obviously it's not enough just to read about an artwork in a book to appreciate it properly. The point is that ordinarily these presuppositions are *tacit* – we take them for granted rather like we take much of our everyday experience for granted.

Think back to our discussion in Chapter one of conceptual analysis, and the analogy we drew there with consciousness. Just as we may not know what art is, but whatever it is, *Birth of Venus* is art for sure, so you may not know exactly what consciousness is, but for sure you and your friends are conscious, and sticks and stones are not, whatever the term 'conscious' precisely means. Equally with consciousness, your presuppositions are tacit: you mightn't give it a moment's thought, but still your best friend is *obviously* conscious. But if you were asked to provide a definition of consciousness, you would very likely be stumped for an answer.

Works of conceptual art are in this respect analogous to the Nexus-6 replicants in *Blade Runner* that we discussed in Chapter one. These robots give the impression of being conscious. Yet, we are told, they lack empathy, and they have a fail-safe mechanism of a four-year life span to make sure that they don't develop any such disposition. And so here our intuitions begin to break down, and we are no longer sure what to say about these robots. Are they conscious or not? In these uncharted waters, we have to do some careful thinking, because the answers to our questions have important practical implications.

Analogously, thinking about conceptual art leads us to ask whether Vito Acconci's *Following Piece*, or Duchamp's *Fountain*, really is art. If it is art, then what is the artwork, and where does it begin and end, so to speak? What is more, once we can say what the artwork is, how are we to appreciate it as art? With conceptual art, obvious answers don't come readily to hand as they do with *Birth of Venus*; and if they do we might worry that our answers are just expressions of prejudice. If we are right in our claim that the answers to our definitional, ontological and epistemological questions matter here, we must begin looking for the answers. We start with the question of definition.

DEFINITION: IS IT ART?

There are a number of reasons why defining art might seem unimportant or irrelevant. One such reason which we have just touched on is this: we don't seem to care about definitions with traditional art so why should it be such a big deal when we turn to conceptual art? We've already made some progress in addressing this: we *do* care, although we simply don't think about it.

Another thought, in roughly the same territory, will lead us to the first approach to the definition of art that we want to consider. It is based on the elusive character of conceptual art that we raised in Chapter one, and has been put very succinctly by the philosopher Jerrold Levinson:

> If one reflects on the varieties of art and art making in the past half century, one cannot help but be struck by the fact that, intrinsically speaking, there are simply no holds barred. Anything, seen from outside as it were, *can* be art. At the same time, that hardly means that. . . there is no distinction worth capturing, and yet we would be profoundly dissatisfied to learn that all that remained of arthood was a purely trivial marker such as the condition of having been *called* or *dubbed* "art". Still, on the other hand, the return to a traditional notion of aesthetic aim or aesthetic experience seems blocked by the undeniable evolution of art beyond this sort of contemplative, perceptually based conception, as evidenced [amongst others] by Conceptual Art . . .[24]

What are we to say here? Perhaps art simply can't be defined.

RESISTING DEFINITION

Surprisingly perhaps, this thought, that art can't be defined, may be better grounded than one might suspect at first glance. Several philosophers have argued in defence of the claim that certain concepts – concepts we all use and feel familiar with – just can't be defined. For example, the term 'sport' can rightly be applied to many activities, some of which will involve balls, and others not, some of which will require a team, and others not, some of which will take place in water, and others not, and so on. Similarly, the term 'game' is quite 'open' so to speak, since a game can be something that involves dice, or not, or which requires cards, or not, and so on. The thought here is that it is difficult, if not impossible, to capture the notion of 'sport' or 'game' within a single, simple definition. If this is true, then how can we account for the fact that most of us do, nonetheless, seem to have at least a relatively good grasp of what counts as a sport or game, and what does not? We know that javelin-throwing is a sport whereas cooking isn't. We know that gin rummy is a game but that Tarot isn't. And of course, the same questions come up with art.

First, though, let's take a closer look at the claim that certain concepts cannot be defined. What does it actually mean? When philosophers argue that X (sport, game, art) cannot be defined, what they have in mind is that it isn't possible to give a set of *necessary and sufficient conditions* that all, and only, Xs will satisfy. A *necessary* condition for something to be an X is a condition that that thing *has* to meet in order to qualify as an X; in other words, if it doesn't meet that condition, then it's not an X. A *sufficient* condition is a condition such that, if something has it, then it will qualify as an X.

An example from a different context can illustrate the idea. To be a person who is allowed to vote in a national election in the UK, it's necessary to be eighteen years old or over. But this is not a sufficient condition. For if you are eighteen or over and not resident, or in prison, then you aren't allowed to vote. So, in order to be allowed to vote, you must satisfy the set of necessary conditions (of which these are just three), which, together, are *jointly sufficient* for you to be allowed to vote.[25]

Intuitively, there might seem to be something appealing about the idea that art resists definition (now understood as the idea that there is no set of *individually necessary and jointly sufficient conditions* for something to be an artwork). For the very idea of definition might seem to preclude the possibility of innovation – innovation of just the kind that we find in conceptual art, and (although perhaps less radically) throughout the history of art. The philosopher Morris Weitz, an important proponent of this view, argued very much along these lines. Writing in the 1950s, he said this:

> "Art", itself, is an open concept. New conditions (cases) have constantly arisen and will undoubtedly constantly arise; new art forms, new movements will emerge, which will demand decisions on the part of those interested, usually professional critics, as to whether the concept should be extended or not. Aestheticians may lay down similarity conditions but never necessary and sufficient ones for the correct application of the concept. With "art" its conditions of application can never be exhaustively enumerated since new cases can always be envisaged or created by artists, or even nature, which would call for a decision of someone's part to extend or to close the old or to invent a new concept. . . . What I am arguing, then, is that the very expansive, adventurous character of art, its ever-present changes and novel creations makes it logically impossible to ensure any set of defining properties.[26]

This echoes Levinson's worry. But what does Weitz put in the place of what he thinks is the chimera of definition? For after all, there must be *something* in virtue of which we are able to distinguish art from non-art. Weitz advocates that we just 'look and see'. In practice, he claims, we have no trouble in distinguishing art from non-art – we do so merely by looking, or, more generally, by perceiving. In support of this, another philosopher, William Kennick, also writing in the 1950s, asks us to imagine a warehouse 'filled with all sorts of things – pictures of every description, musical scores . . . machines, tools, boats, houses, churches and temples, statues, vases, books of poetry and prose, furniture and clothing, newspapers, postage stamps, flowers, trees, stones, musical instruments'.[27] Someone who is asked to bring out all the works of art the warehouse contains will, he claims, 'be able to do this with reasonable success', just by looking and seeing. There is, then, no great mystery about identifying things that resist definition.

In the spirit of Ludwig Wittgenstein, Weitz and Kennick appeal to the idea of *perceptible family resemblance*. The thought is that members of a family share certain perceptible features (length of nose, colour of hair, size of feet, and so on), even though there is no single feature or group of perceptible features which is definitive of, or necessary and sufficient for, being a member of that family. What we do, they suggest, is pick out certain things as belonging to a certain category, such as belonging to a certain family, in virtue of their 'resembling' other things that we know for sure belong to that category. So if we are looking at an object and wondering if it should be classified as a work of art, we look to other similar things that we know to be paradigmatic cases of art, and check whether the first object shares some of the properties with the second object. If it does, we call it a work of art.

Appealing as this view might be at first glance, there are a number of difficulties with it. We will discuss just two.[28]

First, we can somewhat turn the tables on Weitz and Kennick and say that their proposed solution, allegedly capable of accommodating what Weitz refers to as 'the very expansive, adventurous character of art', in fact has the opposite effect. To use an example we are familiar with, Duchamp's *Fountain* bears no *perceptible* resemblance at all to what had gone before it in art history, which indicates that perceptible resemblance doesn't seem to be *necessary* for something to qualify as art. Perceptible resemblance might accommodate developments out of an existing tradition or within one and the same art movement, but it won't be able to make room for the kind of explosive revolution exemplified by *Fountain*, and by much conceptual art since then. Of course one might insist here that *Fountain* after all really *isn't* art, so it doesn't represent a counterexample to the perceptual resemblance account. Perhaps, but it's important to appreciate that this would fly in the face of the idea that the perceptible resemblance account is able to accommodate 'the very expansive, adventurous character of art'.

Nor does perceptible resemblance seem to be a *sufficient* condition for something's being art. Duchamp's *Fountain* bears a strong resemblance to all those other non-artwork urinals from which just this one was chosen by Duchamp; and Andy Warhol's *Brillo Boxes* look indistinguishable from the Brillo boxes that you could find in the supermarket. And yet it is agreed on all sides that these *other* urinals and Brillo boxes are not works of art.

On reflection, there really is something rather odd in the fact that proponents of this view should have chosen perceptible *family* resemblance as one of its leading examples. For perceptible resemblance isn't necessary for being a member of a family. Mrs Jones' daughter might not look *at all* like Mrs Jones, but she is still Mrs Jones' daughter. And perceptible resemblance isn't sufficient for being a member of a family. Mrs Jones' daughter might look just like the daughter of the Queen of England but this doesn't make her a member of the Royal Family. Arthur Danto, one of its fiercest critics, describes the appeal to family resemblance as 'almost appallingly ill-chosen'.[29]

In order to undermine Weitz's and Kennick's idea that we can tell art from non-art by 'looking and seeing', we can consider Danto's idea of *indiscernibles*, which we briefly encountered in Chapter one. Danto imagines what he calls a 'counterwarehouse', in which all those things that were art in the first warehouse are now not art, and all those things that weren't art are now art. Now, with examples such as *Fountain* and *Brillo Boxes* in mind, it is surely right, as Danto claims, that the man asked to bring out all the works of art would not be able to tell art from non-art *just by looking*. Recent art (including conceptual art as well as much else besides) has helped to make this idea of what Danto calls the 'transfiguration of the commonplace' very familiar to all of us. We leave it to the reader to think of recent works such as piles of stones, flowers, sheds, newspapers and boats. Similarly, thinking of Martin Creed's Turner Prize-winning entry for 2001, *Work No 227, The Lights Going On and Off* (Figure 2.1), we might even now add that the Creed warehouse has a Creed-like non-art counter-warehouse with some faulty wiring causing the lights to go on and off. So even the warehouse itself, as well as its contents, serves to show that the perceptible resemblance account is a failure.

The first difficulty with the perceptible family resemblance account, which conceptual art reveals particularly clearly, can be summed up as follows: something's having a perceptible resemblance to the art that has preceded it is neither necessary nor sufficient for that thing to qualify as art.

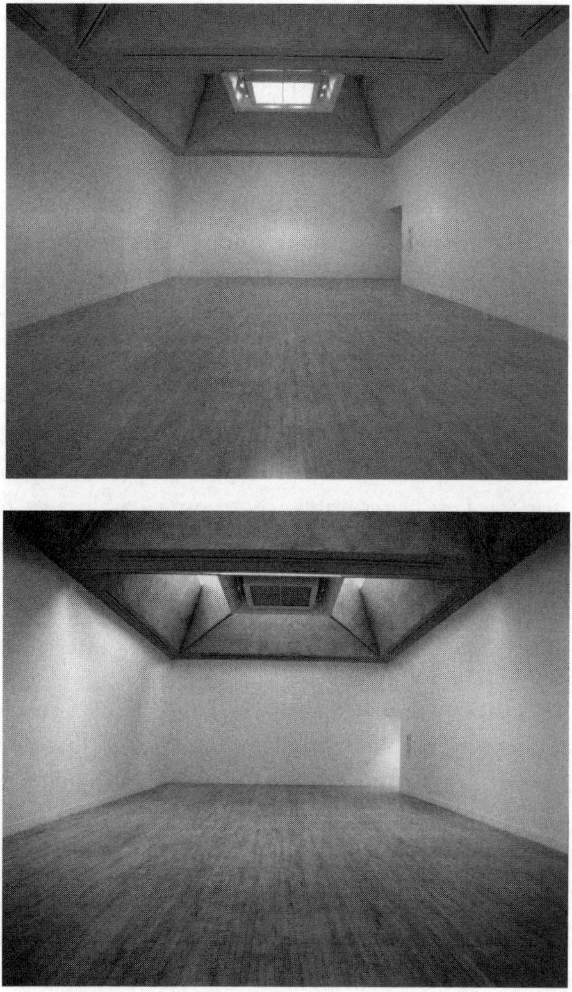

Figure 2.1 (a,b) Martin Creed, *The Lights Going On and Off*.

Martin CREED Work No. 227: The lights going on and off 2000
5 seconds on, 5 seconds off
Installation view at TATE Britain, London/UK

Photo: Tate Photography
Courtesy the artist and Hauser & Wirth Zürich London

We can be very brief with the second difficulty. One of the principal motivations for the family resemblance account was that all other definitions of art that seek to provide necessary and sufficient conditions for something being a work of art preclude the possibility of innovation in art. But this isn't so. For example, an idea that has appealed to many conceptual artists is that they, the artists, are amongst the people who can decide what is art – remember here Donald Judd's saying, 'if someone calls it art, it's art'. So if this were right, an artist could produce something highly innovative and then call it art, and he would thereby have created an artwork: calling it art is sufficient (and let's assume also necessary) for something's being an artwork. Thus one of the principal motivations for the family resemblance account has lost its force: innovation in art is consistent with art having necessary and sufficient conditions.

ART DEFINED INSTITUTIONALLY

Let's pick up on the last idea, which will lead us into a discussion of the second kind of definition of art that we want to consider – one that has been enduringly popular in one form or other, namely the so-called *institutional theory* of art. Here is a formulation of the institutional theory by one of its main proponents, the philosopher George Dickie: the idea, roughly, is that it is artists who create art, to be presented to the 'artworld public'. The five following conditions, Dickie tells us, are each necessary, and jointly sufficient, for something's being an artwork:

1. An artist is a person who participates with understanding in the making of a work of art.

2. A work of art is an artefact of a kind created to be presented to an artworld public.
3. A public is a set of persons the members of which are prepared in some degree to understand an object which is presented to them.
4. The artworld is the totality of all artworld systems.
5. An artworld system is a framework for the presentation of a work of art by an artist to an artworld.[30]

We can't possibly address all the issues that arise in relation to the institutional theory here. The important thing is to see its implications for conceptual art. First, there's a common misunderstanding of the institutional theory which arises from some of its earlier formulations, that the status of being an artwork is conferred by the 'artworld' rather like one might name a ship or promote someone to Captain. On this interpretation, *Fountain* and *Blue Plaque* wouldn't be works of art when Duchamp and Turk presented their work to, respectively, the directors of the Society of Independent Artists and the examiners of the Royal College of Art. For the 'artworld', if that was what these august and knowledgeable people represented, *rejected* the pieces. This would be unfortunate, not only in these cases, but also in a case where the artist in his lonely atelier has, we surely want to say, made a work of art *before* it's seen and 'given the nod' by the artworld public. The artwork is there, with its status already in place, for the public to *discover*.

The second point is that the definition of art according to the institutional theory is entirely non-judgemental – bad art is as much art as good art: all that's necessary is that the artwork be created 'to be presented to an artworld public'. However, the artist must, roughly, know what he or she is doing, be someone who 'participates with understanding'. To put it simply, not anyone is an artist just because they *claim* to be one, or because they crudely imitate the behaviour of the real artist. So the toddler saying 'Look, Mummy, I'm an artist' as she daubs paint on the paper doesn't thereby turn herself into an artist.

According to the institutional definition, then, the artwork has to be created by the artist with the aim in mind that it be an artwork. But we've now seen that this is really quite a minimal condition. For example, many traditional pictures have been painted with the further aim of giving rise to pleasure in the viewer, or with the further aim of expressing or communicating certain feelings; to this extent at least some art does seem to have a kind of function. And yet, according to the institutional theory, these further aims are by no means necessary for something's being a work of art. What we have here, it seems, is a clash between an attempt at defining art in *procedural* terms (institutional theory) and another attempt at defining art in *functional* terms. Let's turn to this second kind of definition.

ART DEFINED FUNCTIONALLY

A functional definition defines something in terms of what it is meant or intended to do. For example, a functional definition of a knife is one given in terms of the knife's purpose, namely cutting. What, then, might be the function of art? Perhaps its function is, very roughly, to fulfil some kind of human need or concern.[31] There are, not surprisingly, many views here about how to fill in the crucial detail, but the general idea is that we value art if it performs its function well: perhaps to express or communicate certain feelings or to give rise to a certain kind of pleasure in the spectator on perceptual encounter with it. Yet much modern art, of which conceptual art is very much an instance in this respect, doesn't seem to have a function of this kind.[32] We've already seen in Chapter one how conceptual art eschews the aesthetic, and the expression or communication of feelings or emotions isn't what conceptual art is about either. This is why, according to most functional definitions of art, conceptual art would fail to be art.

However, stripping from the definition of art all reference to its function (such as the function of giving rise to certain kinds of experience) isn't the only way to accommodate conceptual art as art. Here are two others. First, one might *reinterpret* the traditional function. This might be done by extending the traditional notion of the aesthetic (a notion which we have so far carefully left undefined in a precise way) to include aesthetic *ideas*. This will be the topic of Chapter four. Or one might give art some kind of intellectual function, such as the communication of intellectual ideas and emotions. This will be the topic of Chapter five.

A second way of accommodating conceptual art as art, still whilst holding onto a functional definition, is to provide a definition of art according to which something is art if it meets one or more (but not necessarily all) of a set of conditions, some of which involve reference to functional properties, and others not. Different versions of this kind of account have been argued for recently; whilst they are worth exploring, this book isn't the place to start, for it will divert us from our main aims.[33]

SO IS 'CONCEPTUAL ART' ART?

There are (at least) two possible answers to this question. One possible answer is that conceptual art is indeed art. Philosophers' definitions of art now satisfactorily accommodate conceptual art (after making accommodating revisions to catch up with progress in the artworld). But our everyday commonsense notion of art hasn't yet caught up with the philosophers and the artworld: this unreflective notion remains loyal to the traditional functional definition of art, and thus excludes conceptual art. And this, perhaps, might explain why so many of us – let's call them the *sceptics* – don't appreciate conceptual art. The question 'But is it art?' meets with a firm 'No' from the sceptic, and it meets with this response just because conceptual art fails to meet the traditionally understood function of art, such as the creation of aesthetic pleasure, or the communication of feelings. Conceptual art might be accepted as art by the 'artworld', but the sceptic, in the spirit of Tom Wolfe, will see this as part of a conspiracy. So if a sceptic is confronted with a clutch of artists and art critics, all members of the artworld, and all insisting that the latest offering really is art, she will simply reply, in the spirit of conspiracy theorists everywhere, 'Well, they would say that, wouldn't they?'. The emperor has no clothes, she says, but, as in the fable, the emperor's nudity is wilfully not noticed by everyone else. But, according to this answer, the sceptic is wrong; she needs to catch up with reality – the world has changed.

A second possible answer is to insist that the sceptic is right: conceptual art really *isn't* art. According to this view, there is a true functional definition of art, arrived at after careful philosophical reflection, and which incorporates, let us say, the traditional notion that the function of art is to provide aesthetic pleasure. And conceptual art fails – *wilfully* fails we might add – to satisfy that definition.

On either of these two possible answers, the explanation of the sceptic's difficulties with conceptual art lies in an implicit understanding of the definition of art as embodying some kind of function or aim, understood in the traditional way.[34] The disagreement, between sceptic and non-sceptic, then comes down to deciding whether or not this definition of art is the right one, and thus over whether the sceptic's skepticism is warranted.

You'll recall from Chapter one that one of the typical characteristics of conceptual art is that it is against definition. We can now see that it's anti-definition in two ways. First, it rejects the idea that the question of whether or not conceptual art is art is a question to be arbitrated by someone other than the artist himself or herself. Second, it rejects the deeply rooted intuitive definition of art, as grounded in the idea that there is some traditionally-minded function or aim, perhaps aesthetic, that all art is supposed to satisfy. Hopefully we have shown how these two ways of being anti-definition are related, and that the approach of each of us to conceptual art can't be entirely neutral about the question of definition.

We won't decide on these difficult questions here, leaving them for you to ponder – questions about the definition of art, and questions about whether it is concerns about definition that explain the sceptic's scepticism, the doubters' doubts, the fearer's fears. For it's now time to consider questions about ontology. Perhaps it is the strange ontology of conceptual art that explains the scepticism, the doubts, the fears.

ONTOLOGY: WHERE IS THE ARTWORK?

As we explained in Chapter one, ontology is concerned, roughly, with what there is. Understood in this way, one aspect of ontology addresses questions of whether or not something exists. This aspect isn't our concern here. We are interested in another aspect of ontology, one that addresses questions concerning things that *do* exist – questions, for example, about the nature of their existence, their properties and their relations to other things that exist. Relating this to our subject matter of art, we start with the presupposition that there are such things as artworks, concerning ourselves with what kinds of things artworks are, what properties they can have, and how they can relate to other things, including the psychology of people.

ARE ARTWORKS THINGS?

Even at this very general ontological level, it's important to appreciate that the notion of 'thing' and of 'something' has to be taken in as wide a sense as possible when we ask the question 'What kind of thing is a work of art?'. In other words, we don't want a notion of 'thing' which just includes 'things' that have a size, shape and location such as tables and chairs. We should leave open the possibility that artworks can also include, for example, 'things' such as events, thoughts, ideas, and abstract objects. All these are things too, even though they aren't spatio-temporal objects.[35]

In this wide sense of the term 'thing', works of conceptual art will undoubtedly be things – after all, they *exist* (remember this is what we are presupposing). This is why it would be misleading to say that conceptual art is anti-ontology (indeed, this isn't an easy 'ology to be anti). But we should not presuppose that they are things in the narrow sense of the term – in other words, that they are spatio-temporal objects; we began to undermine that idea in Chapter one. Moreover, we shouldn't even presuppose that *traditional* artworks, such as sculptures, pictures, and other examples of what are called the *plastic arts*, are spatio-temporal objects. This may seem surprising and counterintuitive, but thinking about the ontology of some strange works of conceptual art might lead us to revise our intuitive thinking about the ontology of traditional art too.

THE ART MEDIUM

To begin with, let's consider for a moment the point of view of a traditional artist when he goes about 'making' or 'creating' a work of art. The artist might begin with a certain aim, let's say to portray a likeness of The President of the United States. He then decides how he is going to set about this task, and in particular what medium he will use to achieve his aim. Will it be a picture or will it be a sculpture? If the former, will it be a lithograph, an oil painting, or etching? If the latter, will it be worked in bronze, in marble, or what? What size will it be? There will be a myriad of such questions for the artist to answer in what we might call the planning stage, before he begins his work – that is to say, before he begins to work the chosen material, to apply paint to canvas, chisel to marble, and so on. The answers to his myriad questions will depend on all sorts of things: the particular skill of the artist; the material that is available and affordable; the suitability of the material to the subject to be portrayed; the preferences of the patron and the preferences and character of the sitter; the current fashion, artistic convention, and so on and so forth. The answers in many cases will be taken for granted – Canova might not consciously consider painting in oils, Velasquez will think of this first, and so on.

So for each traditional artwork, there is a *medium* in which that work will be made. And, moreover, for each *art form* – sculpture, painting and so forth – there is a limited range of media which are 'proper' to it. This is what we called *medium specificity* in Chapter one. Traditionally, artists are trained to develop their skills to work in a particular medium, although some, of course, will be skilled in more than one. The idea of a medium suggests some kind of mediation or communication. Traditionally in art, the artist uses a *physical* medium –

the paint, the canvas, and so forth which he works on in a particular way – as the means to communicate what he or she wants to communicate; and, correlatively, this medium is the means by which our appreciation of the artist's artistic statement is mediated.

The idea might seem complicated, but really it's very simple. Consider an analogy. A friend of yours has just passed her exams, and you want to communicate your congratulations to her. 'How should I do this?' you ask yourself. 'By phone, by email, by handwritten or typed letter, by sending flowers, by text message, in person?' and what words should you use, or should you use some other means and give her a hug? These are some of the means that you might use to communicate your thoughts and feelings.

This analogy shows two things about the medium of communication. First, there are better and worse choices of medium in a particular case. And second, a gap can easily open up between the thoughts and feelings that you intend to convey and what you actually did convey – the words can be misunderstood, the hug taken as something quite different.

And in art too, gaps open up, as we all know. In the late eighteenth century, the sculptor Etienne Falconnet, after years of effort, finished his massive sculpture of Peter the Great of Russia in St Petersburg. It was commissioned by Catherine the Great with the requirement that Falconnet communicate Peter's enormous power (and hers too by inheritance) as supreme ruler of all Russia. But, at least on many accounts, Falconnet didn't achieve this aim: the size of the sculpture, which is now fondly known as the *Bronze Horseman* after the poem by Pushkin, just makes Peter look *big*.[36] This illustrates the point that the skill of an artist isn't just in having a wonderfully conceived artistic aim, but also in executing that conception in the chosen physical medium in a way that best communicates it. The proper execution of the aim is an essential ingredient for success in communication. Jonathan Richardson, in his *An Essay on the Theory of Painting*, written in 1715, summarises it thus:

> In all the works of art there is to be considered the thought, and the workmanship, or manner of expressing or executing that thought. What ideas the artist had we can only guess at by what we see, and consequently cannot tell how far he has fallen short, or perhaps by accident exceeded them, but the work, like the corporeal and material part of man, is apparent, and to be seen to the utmost. Thus, in the art I am discoursing upon, everything that is done is in pursuance of some ideas the master has, whether he can reach with his hand what his mind has conceived, or no.[37]

To put Richardson's point in a nutshell, the work, including the manifest workmanship, is all we have to go on to establish what the artist's thought was 'behind' the work. Perhaps the artist struck lucky and achieved *more* than he or she aimed at; or perhaps success was only partial. But in any event, it is the work, the work worked in a physical medium, which is the means by which the artist communicates, more or less successfully, his or her ideas. If there's no work in a physical medium, then there's no communication; that is to say, a physical medium is necessary for the artist to communicate his or her ideas.

THE ONTOLOGICAL CHALLENGE FROM CONCEPTUAL ART: THE IDEA IDEA

How does conceptual art challenge these ontological intuitions exemplified by centuries of traditional artworks, and so clearly set out by Richardson? They are rejected by conceptual artists through the *idea idea*, which we first introduced in

Chapter one. We need now to make sense of this rejection, and to see its ontological implications (and, in due course, its implications for how we go about appreciating conceptual art). Here are citations from two conceptual artists that give expression to the idea idea:

Joseph Kosuth:

> Conceptual art, simply put, has as its basic tenet an understanding that artists work with meaning, not with shapes, colours, or materials.[38]
>
> The "art idea" and art are the same.[39]

Sol LeWitt:

> In conceptual art the idea or concept is the most important aspect of the work. When an artist uses a conceptual form of art, it means that all of the planning and decisions are made beforehand and the execution is a perfunctory affair.[40]
>
> Ideas can be works of art. . . . All ideas need not be made physical.[41]

In Chapter one we saw just this kind of example at the end of Tom Wolfe's *The Painted Word*, of the 'work' by Lawrence Weiner. You'll recall from Chapter one that all there is to the 'work' is a piece of paper on the wall, with these words:

> 1. The artist may construct the piece
> 2. The piece may be fabricated
> 3. The piece may not be built
>
> Each being equal and consistent with the intent of the artist the decision as to condition rests with the receiver upon the occasion of receivership.[42]

It's beginning to seem as if we were wrong: the *idea* of communicating your congratulations to your friend is all you need. No need to worry about the execution (that's a 'perfunctory affair'). Or alternatively, you could get someone else to communicate your congratulations for you ('the piece may be fabricated'). But leaving the analogy before it gets overstrained, let's return to the challenge from conceptual art to our implicit, intuitive ontology of art. It comes in four parts, each of which has increasingly important implications for our appreciation of conceptual art as art.

First, there is the rejection of *medium-specificity*. When conceptual art has some kind of physical presence (which certainly can be the case), this need not involve any particular means of production. In this it can be seen as something of a direct reaction against modernism. Clement Greenberg, the modernist critic whom we encountered in Chapter one, saw the task of each art form to manifest, to express, to *celebrate* its own essence – the essence of painting, for example, being flatness. Tom Wolfe thought that this was bound to lead to a dead end.

The second ontological challenge from conceptual art is that, when we do have a physical presence, it often falls well short of being a suitable object for appreciation, at least in the traditional sense: the typed sheet from Weiner; the urinal from Duchamp (Figure 1.3); the blown-up photograph of a dictionary definition of water from Joseph Kosuth (Figure 1.6). Are these the physical things that we are supposed to stand and admire, in *just the same way* as we stand and admire a Botticelli or a Vermeer? Surely this would be a mistake. But if so, what *are* we supposed to do if we want to appreciate conceptual art?

Third, there is *dematerialisation* – so nicely mocked in the wall drawing by Dan Perjovschi at MoMA (Figure 2.2).[43] Two

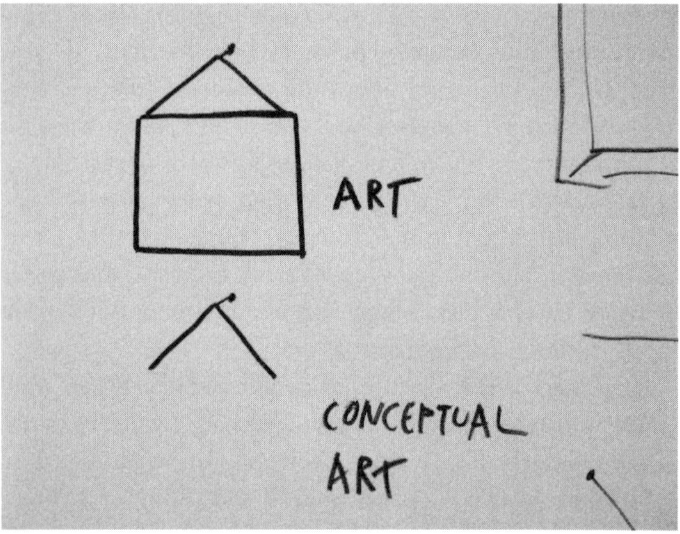

Figure 2.2 Dan Perjovschi, Wall at MoMA.
Dan Perjovschi "What Happen to US?" Project 85, 2007, permanet marker on wall, MoMA New York, photo? . . . courtesy the artist, MoMA and Lombard-Freod Projects © Taís Melillo

works, both by Robert Barry, illustrate (if that is the right term here) dematerialisation. In his *Inert Gas Series*, one titled *Inert Gas: Helium* (Figure 2.3), Barry released small amounts of helium in a California desert, 'sometime during the morning of March 4, 1969'. As Barry himself said, 'inert gas is a material that is imperceptible . . . It continues to expand forever in the atmosphere, constantly changing, and it does all of this without anybody being able to see it'.[44] The second work consists of Barry's words, written on a wall in New York City, *All the things I know but of which I am not at the moment thinking*, 1.36 pm June 15, 1969. That's it, that's the artwork. When we are faced with dematerialisation in this sense, we seem to have no *object* to appreciate – nothing, no thing. As Barry said in an interview

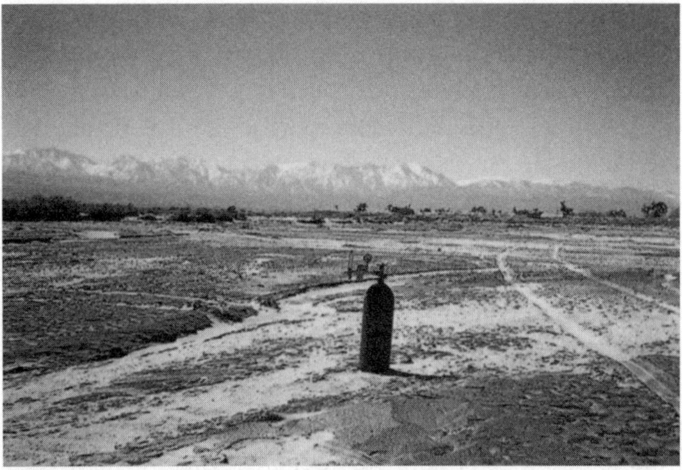

Figure 2.3 Robert Barry, *Inert Gas: Helium.*

RobertBarry, *Inert Gas: Helium* Courtesy the artist

in 1969, 'There are no collectors, for there is nothing to collect'. Thus there is, as Wolfe put it in his discussion of the artwork by Weiner, 'no visual experience before or after whatsoever', which might be seen as a triumph of dematerialisation.

This third challenge from conceptual art to our intuitive ontology of art can be summed up by what Lucy Lippard and John Chandler wrote in 1968:

> During the 1960s, the anti-intellectual, emotional/intuitive processes of art-making of the last two decades have begun to give way to an ultra-conceptual art that emphasizes the thinking processes almost exclusively . . . Such a trend appears to be provoking a profound dematerialisation of art, especially of art as object, and if it continues to prevail, it may result in the object's becoming wholly obsolete.[45]

The fourth challenge from conceptual art leads us back to the idea idea. One way of interpreting Joseph Kosuth's remark that conceptual artists work with meaning and not with shapes, colours, or materials is that conceptual art involves no physical presence at all. But this would be to exclude too much from conceptual art. It would even exclude Robert Barry's *All the things I know*, which, after all, involves *something* physical, namely the words written on the wall in New York City. And it would exclude many other works besides, from Duchamp's *Fountain* onwards.

However, there's another way in which we can understand dematerialisation, and the remark of Kosuth, which eliminates from the work everything physical, even where we have such things as writing on a wall. We can do so by returning to the distinction which we very briefly introduced in Chapter one, between physical medium and physical means. When we used the term 'physical presence' just now, this was intended to be neutral as between physical medium and means, and it allows us to say that conceptual art has no physical *medium*: the medium of conceptual art is ideas, and any physical presence is *merely the means* by which the artist lets us gain access to his ideas. The words that Barry wrote on the wall are merely the means by which we can gain access to the idea, and it is the idea that is the medium. Thus we can make sense not only of Kosuth's remark, but of Sol le Witt's too, that all ideas need not be made physical.

The idea idea, thus understood, is that conceptual art works with ideas, or with concepts, as the medium, and not with shapes, colours, or materials. This, we think, is what marks out conceptual art as *radically* different from traditional art.

WHERE WE'VE BEEN AND WHERE WE'RE GOING

These ontological challenges, very much like the definitional challenges that we looked at earlier in this chapter, raise profoundly difficult questions about the proper appreciation of conceptual art – a question for Chapter three and beyond. But more than that, they also help us to understand the definitional and ontological presuppositions that lie beneath the surface of our appreciation of traditional art, including modernist art.[46]

We'll begin Chapter three by delving a little deeper into the murky waters of ontology, and discuss in more detail the distinction between medium and mere means, which will enable us to understand better how to go about appreciating conceptual art whilst being faithful to its spirit, to the *idea idea*. In particular, we will begin to get to grips with how conceptual art might come to be appreciated, and appreciated *as art*, when it seems to be so patently lacking in aesthetic aim in anything like the traditional sense.

Appreciating Conceptual Art

Three

INTRODUCTION

At the heart of this chapter is the notion of the artistic appreciation of conceptual art. How are we to perceive, assess, and enjoy conceptual art, given that it has no physical medium? What should we look out for, and by what criteria should we judge it? Providing answers to these questions is in the service of the question of appreciation of art which has the idea idea at its heart.

We have now established that, at least most of the time, we feel at home with traditional art. We know where we are: we know that traditional art is indeed art (*definition*); we know what the artwork is (*ontology*); we know how to go about appreciating it (*epistemology*); and, more or less, we know what its value is – what sort of properties of traditional art are proper objects of appreciation (including in particular its *aesthetic* properties). Recall Botticelli's *Birth ofVenus*: we know that it's art; we know that it's the *picture* that is the object of appreciation; we know that we need to look at it (front on etc) if we are to appreciate it; and we also know that our appreciation will be centred on the aesthetic properties of the picture, often attested by the feeling of pleasure or delight that we get from contemplating it.

These intuitive commonsense ideas about art have no doubt been shaped by our idea of *fine art*. This idea really only developed in Western Europe in the eighteenth century, when, it was thought, there were just five kinds of fine art (pictures, architecture, music, poetry and sculpture), each with its own medium, and each with its own epistemology.[47] Now, faced with conceptual art, we find ourselves in uncharted definitional, ontological, epistemological and evaluative waters – adrift too, without a point where we can firmly make anchor in order to get our bearings in our unfamiliar surroundings. Remember Dan Perjovschi's wall drawing (Figure 2.2), which nicely captures the unsettling doubts and fears of the unknown: the familiar picture has disappeared and nothing is there to replace it – nothing physical.

All of this can be very disturbing when it comes to the question of how we are to appreciate conceptual art, and perhaps that is why so many of us are sceptical or have doubts about it, and why we often feel threatened or sometimes even offended when confronted by conceptual art. Are we still 'burdened' with these 'commonsense' ideas about art, which worked perfectly well in the eighteenth century, and which still work perfectly well with traditional art? Or are there other, perhaps more subtle, explanations of our scepticism, our doubts, our fears? We need to revisit in greater detail our ontological presuppositions about traditional art that we began to discuss in Chapter two.

THE OBJECT MODEL

Let's begin by returning to a question that we have already raised: Is it really so very clear that our commonsense ontology of art always selects a *physical object* for appreciation, and if so *only* a physical object? We'll call the view that answers this question in the affirmative the *object model*.

Let's consider paintings, where perhaps our intuitions about the object model might seem to be most firmly embedded. Now, on deeper reflection, when we consider paintings – those 'things on the wall' which we find in art galleries and museums and which seem at first paradigmatically to fit the object model – the model really doesn't turn out to apply in such a clear-cut way. For it seems that it isn't *only* the object, the physical object, that we pick out for appreciation.

Consider the following example. Imagine that you go to an exhibition and see a scroll exhibited on the wall with some writing on it in a language which is unfamiliar to you – Japanese say. How should you appreciate the scroll? In order to appreciate it, we need to know whether what we are looking at is a piece of calligraphy, or a poem. Putting the point rather too simply perhaps, if it is a piece of calligraphy, the content of what is written (what the words mean) is not relevant for appreciation, but only the way and technique with which it is written (remember here your handwriting lessons at school). In contrast, if it is a poem, the content is relevant, but not the way in which it is written. However, if it is both calligraphy and poem, then both content and manner of writing are relevant. So if we want properly to appreciate this work, it's not sufficient for us to pick out the physical object as the thing to appreciate, as *the work of art*, which is what the object model insists on. We need also to know what kind of art it is, or to which *category* it belongs, and this isn't always apparent merely from a visual inspection of the physical object.[48]

We might, then, have to amend the object model so that our commonsense ontology of art (pictorial art) picks out a physical object for appreciation, but with the proviso that we also need to know what category of art the object falls under. But now, here is a further step that we want to take in undermining the object model, even in this revised form. We want to show that it is also highly relevant for the appreciation of an artwork what the story is 'behind' it, in terms of how and why the artwork came about. We will call this the *narrative of the work*, or the *work-narrative*.

THE WORK-NARRATIVE

A narrative, roughly, is an account or explanation of events. It not only reveals causal connections between these events, but also shows them to have a certain coherence, to make sense both to those who are 'internal' to the narrative, and to those to whom the narrative might be addressed. In the context of artworks, a work-narrative is a narrative of the events surrounding and leading up to the creation of the work as we experience it.[49] (This idea of a work-narrative is meant to be neutral with regards to other aspects of the ontology of the artwork – whether, for example, the medium is a physical object or something else, such as a sequence of events or sounds, or, as is the case with conceptual art, ideas. We will return to this shortly.)

The idea of the perfect copy illustrates the importance of a work-narrative in our appreciation of a picture. The perfect copy is, by assumption, perceptually indistinguishable in all respects from the original: it *looks* or *appears* just the same. But we appreciate the two works differently, and we do this at least partly because they have different work-narratives. That is to say, not only the historical context but also the motivation and thought-processes that lead up to the making of the artwork are very different, for whilst the artist who made the original set out to create an original work of art, the copyist is just trying to make a perfect copy.

But we don't need the thought experiment of a perfect copy to show why the work-narrative matters. In fact, many works of conceptual art will do the job for us much better. Let's consider a marvellous work of Duchamp, *LHOOQ Shaved*. To understand it, we need first to understand an earlier work of Duchamp, namely *LHOOQ* (Figure 3.1), a cheap reproduction of the *Mona Lisa* to which Duchamp has added a moustache and goatee beard. This is what Duchamp said about it:

> This Mona Lisa with a moustache and a goatee is a combination readymade and iconoclastic Dadaism. The original, I mean the original readymade, is a cheap chromo 8x5 on which I inscribed at the bottom four letters which pronounced like initials in French, made a very risqué joke on the Gioconda.[50]

Then we come to his *LHOOQ Shaved*. Here is the philosopher Timothy Binkley's description of how it came to be:

> Duchamp sent out invitations to preview the show . . . On the front of the invitation he pasted a playing card which bears a reproduction of the *Mona Lisa*. Below the card is inscribed, in French, "L.H.O.O.Q. Shaved".

This is very clever. What we have here is something that is perceptually indistinguishable from a reproduction of the *Mona Lisa*; indeed, in a sense that is just what it is. But *LHOOQ Shaved* is different from a mere reproduction of the *Mona Lisa*, not just because it's a numerically different object, but also because the works are different in respect of their work-narratives. Unlike the mere reproduction, *LHOOQ Shaved* is a superbly witty commentary by Duchamp on his earlier work. (In this sense, of course, it nicely manifests one of the typical characteristics of conceptual art that we discussed in Chapter one: ironic self-reflectiveness.)

One might be tempted here to drop the object out of the picture altogether, and insist that all that is of interest is the work-narrative. But this, we think, would be a mistake – one that is often grounded on an epistemological worry.

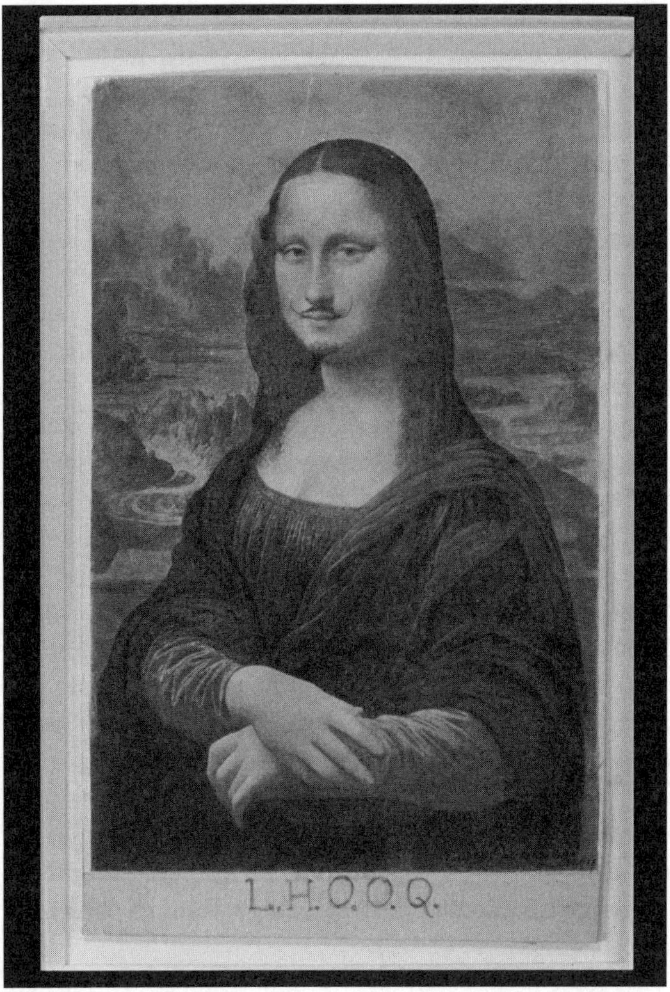

Figure 3.1 Marcel Duchamp, *LHOOQ*.

AN EPISTEMOLOGICAL WORRY

The worry takes us back to the idea of the perfect copy. We might not *know* which is the original work and which is the copy: after all, they are perceptually indistinguishable. Accepting this as a possibility, one might then try in effect to remove the worry by insisting that it doesn't *matter* which is which, just so long as no one finds out. But this further thought is insidious. It's to draw an evaluative conclusion (the difference doesn't matter) from an epistemological premise (we can't tell the difference), and this is something that one cannot do.

To bring the point home, consider an analogy from outside art. You love your partner. Now assume that her doppelganger had been substituted overnight without your noticing, so that your feelings are now directed towards this intruder. In the same spirit as the argument we've just been looking at, you might accept that you've made a mistake, but still insist that it doesn't matter – just so long as you never find out. But surely you love her not only because of how she appears to you perceptually, but also because of your whole history of being together; you love her because it's *her*. Even if this example isn't sufficiently persuasive on its own to *prove* that it matters whether or not it really is her and not her doppelganger, at least it ought to show that it isn't *obvious* that it doesn't matter: the evaluative conclusion doesn't follow from the epistemological premise.[51]

With the perfect copy and the doppelganger in mind, let's return to *LHOOQ Shaved* and the idea of the work-narrative. Again, let's assume that we don't *know* which is which: the Duchamp and the mere reproduction of the *Mona Lisa*. There they are, the two physical objects, side-by-side, perceptually indistinguishable (we must assume here that the title *LHOOQ*

Shaved is omitted). Now we are told the work-narrative, and we are suitably amused. So, the argument goes, surely it is after all the work-narrative on its own that amuses and not work-narrative plus the physical object, for which physical object *LHOOQ Shaved* happens to be is irrelevant to our appreciation. The physical object drops out of the appreciation. But again this is to draw an evaluative conclusion from an epistemological premise. You've *made a mistake* if you confuse the two objects, and if all that mattered to appreciation was the work-narrative, then making a mistake about which object was which would be irrelevant so far as appreciation is concerned.

Our reasoning so far might be thought to lead to a serious problem which we will now need to consider. If what we've said really does capture our ontology of artworks, mightn't it end up that there is, in fact, nothing special about conceptual art? For if the fundamental ontology of the actual *Mona Lisa* turns out to be no different in principle from the fundamental ontology of *LHOOQ Shaved*, aren't both works just the physical object plus the work-narrative? On this story, conceptual art would turn out to be just as familiar to us as the pictures on the walls of the fine art galleries of Europe and North America, and this surely isn't right. Where might there be a difference then?

MEDIUM AND MERE MEANS

Let's return for a moment to the scroll. Whether the work is poetry or calligraphy, our access to the work is gained through looking at the marks on the scroll. In both cases, the marks are the means by which our appreciation of the work in mediated. But doesn't there seem to be a difference in the *way* in which we would look at those marks, depending on whether the work is appreciated as a work of calligraphy or as a poem?

To see why there is indeed such a difference, we need to return to the distinction between medium and mere means. Let's apply this distinction to the scroll. If the work is a poem, then the marks on the page are *merely* the means by which we are able to appreciate the work, and the quality of the care and artistry that was taken in making the marks is irrelevant to our appreciation of the poem as a work of art. In contrast, if the work is a piece of calligraphy, the marks on the page are the medium, and they are themselves directly an object of appreciation, which is achieved through direct perceptual experience of those marks.[52]

So now we can see the way in which conceptual art is radically distinctive in its ontology. When a work of conceptual art presents us with a physical object, such as the *Mona Lisa* reproduction in Duchamp's *LHOOQ Shaved*, the physical object is presented to us *merely* as a means to appreciating the work, rather than as a medium in the full-blooded sense. In the case of *LHOOQ*, the care with which the image of the *Mona Lisa* has been reproduced is no more relevant to our appreciation of the work than would be the care with which a poem had been written on the page.[53]

THE PERCEPTUAL REQUIREMENT

To understand where this discussion is leading us we need to get deeper into the nature and role of perceptual experience in our appreciation of art. Our commonsense idea of art is, as we have already seen, that there is a physical medium by which we appreciate an artwork, and it is the physical medium that we need to directly perceive. Let's call this idea the *perceptual requirement*. This idea is, as we'll see, closely related to the thought that the appropriate appreciation of art necessarily involves so-called *aesthetic* appreciation.

The perceptual requirement finds its voice in these famous remarks of the philosopher Frank Sibley, writing in 1965 (shortly before the official 'dawn' of Conceptual Art):

> It is of importance to note first that, broadly speaking, aesthetics deals with a kind of perception. People have to *see* the grace or unity of a work, *hear* the plaintiveness or frenzy in the music, *notice* the gaudiness of colour scheme, *feel* the power of a novel, its mood, or its uncertainty of tone. They may be struck by these qualities at once, or they may come to perceive them only after repeated viewings, hearings, or readings, and with the help of critics. But unless they do perceive them for themselves, aesthetic enjoyment, appreciation, and judgement are beyond them. Merely to learn from others, on good authority, that the music is serene, the play moving, or the picture unbalanced is of little aesthetic value; the crucial thing is to see, hear, or feel.[54]

This seems just right. Aesthetic experience and aesthetic judgement isn't something that we can just pick up from someone else, or simply make our own on the ground of someone else's experience or judgement. Aesthetic appreciation isn't transferable in that way. For example, if I tell you that *The Deposition* by Sir Anthony van Dyck in the Ashmolean Museum in Oxford is a powerfully moving picture, and you accept the truth of what I have just said, you aren't actually making a genuine aesthetic judgement. Nor can you be said to be undergoing a genuine aesthetic experience of the painting by simply listening to my description of it. (This is also true of plays, films, operas, symphonies, and so on.)

What about conceptual art then? Does the same point apply to it or does it represent a counterexample to the perceptual requirement? In other words, does conceptual art – like other kinds of art – call for a direct first-hand perceptual encounter in order to be appreciated appropriately?

Before turning to this question, though, there is a prior one, which is concerned with the literary arts. We've already seen that poetry, and literature in general is, in a sense, non-perceptual, and if this is right, then conceptual art, if it is a counterexample to the perceptual requirement, won't be the only kind of art that is.[55] But Sibley, in the above citation, seems to think that literature is *not* a counterexample, for he clearly implies that *feeling* the power of a novel is a kind of perception. What is the right thing to say here – what can this notion of *feeling* be doing here, and in what sense is our 'encounter' with literature a kind of perception as Sibley seems to insist?

The idea seems to be that our 'encounter' with a novel, for example, must be first-hand in the sense that our being given a report of what is in the novel, or being given a rough idea of what the story is about, is not sufficient for us to perceive it 'for ourselves' – not sufficient for aesthetic appreciation of the novel. So, although the way the words of the novel look on the page doesn't matter (it's not calligraphy), the precise words used, in their precise order, absolutely do matter. For example, however much we try to tell you what a great novel *Heart of Darkness* is, you won't be able to appreciate its aesthetic merits unless you read it for yourself (or take in the words through some other sense modality). And, from the point of view of the novelist, Joseph Conrad, it isn't enough just to have an idea about writing a novel; the precise words have to be written down before the artist's work is done. This is surely a sensible conclusion.

ANTI-AESTHETIC MEETS ANTI-MEDIUM

Now we have the possibility that there is something special about conceptual art in relation to the perceptual requirement: conceptual art does seem to be a counterexample, and to be so in a way that literature is not. Let's return to *LHOOQ* to see why this is the case.

The philosopher Timothy Binkley sets up the contrast very well between the *Mona Lisa* and *LHOOQ*. He begins with something of an endorsement of what we are calling the perceptual requirement in respect of traditional art, and then shows how *LHOOQ* fails to meet it. (According to Binkley, so much the worse for the perceptual requirement!) This is what he says, and it is worth quoting at some length:

> I could, of course, go on indefinitely describing the look of the *Mona Lisa*, and the fidelity with which your imagination reproduced this look would depend upon such things as how good my description is, how good your imagination is, and chance. Yet regardless of how precise and vivid my description is, one thing it will never do is acquaint you with the painting. You cannot claim to know that work of art on the basis of reading the most exquisite description of it, even though you may learn many interesting things about it. The way you come to know the *Mona Lisa* is by looking at it or by looking at a decent reproduction of it. . . .
>
> Now reconsider the description [by Duchamp, as cited above] of Duchamp's piece: *L.H.O.O.Q.* is a reproduction of the Mona Lisa with a moustache, goatee, and letters added. . . . The description tells you what the work of art is; you now know the piece without actually having seen it (or a reproduction of it). When you do see the artwork there are no surprises: Yes, there is the reproduction of the *Mona Lisa*;

> there is the moustache, the goatee; there are the five letters. When you look at the artwork you learn nothing of artistic consequence which you don't already know from the description Duchamp gives, and for this reason it would be pointless to spend time attending to the piece as a connoisseur would savor a Rembrandt. Just the opposite is true of the *Mona Lisa*. If I tell you it is a painting of a woman with an enigmatic smile, I have told you little about the work of art since the important thing is how it *looks*; and that I can only *show* you, I cannot tell you.
>
> This difference can be elucidated by contrasting ideas and appearances. Some art (a great deal of what is considered traditional art) creates primarily with appearances. To know the art is to know the look of it; and to know that is to experience the look, to perceive the appearance. On the other hand, some art creates primarily with ideas. To know the art is to know the idea; and to know an idea is not necessarily to experience a particular sensation, or even to have some particular experience. This is why you can know L.H.O.O.Q. either by looking at it or by having it described to you. (In fact, the piece might be better or more easily known by description than by perception.)[56]

The central point of Binkley's article (appropriately called 'Piece: Contra Aesthetics') is that we shouldn't think that the notion of the *aesthetic* exhausts the notion of the *artistic*. *LHOOQ* is by no means aesthetic (as Duchamp himself insisted on, you will recall), but this is not to say that it is not art, and that it does not have merit *qua* art. We'll return to this in Chapter four. In particular, we'll look in more detail at just what the notion of the aesthetic is, and whether the notion can, after all, be stretched to capture the possibility that *ideas* (such as those of

Duchamp) can be aesthetic. But for now we can see how conceptual art (and the *idea idea*) is both anti-aesthetic and anti-medium. Its being anti-aesthetic is revealed by the fact that the perceptual requirement doesn't hold, as it seems to do for traditional art. Its being anti-medium is revealed by the fact that the physical means of conveying the idea are *merely* means; they are not the medium in the traditional sense that a medium is what mediates our *aesthetic* appreciation (the precise way in which the oils are worked on the canvas for example).

So perhaps Sol LeWitt was right after all: with conceptual art, the execution really is a 'perfunctory affair'. Instead, it's the idea that matters, and what would be a physical medium in traditional art (such as the reproduction of the *Mona Lisa*) is in conceptual art the *mere means* of getting across the idea to us. This is what Binkley means when he writes 'To know the art is to know the idea'.

There remain two concerns that will occupy us for the rest of this chapter and the next. The first is a return to the question of just how seriously we should take the *idea idea*. The second brings us back to Binkley's central message, namely that the artistic isn't exhausted by the aesthetic.

DEMATERIALISATION REVISITED

It is now beginning to look as if we should be taking the dematerialisation of the art object very seriously indeed. All we need, it seems, is to know the idea, and an idea is by no means an object – a spatio-temporal physical object. Let's revisit, in the light of our recent discussion, the question of whether it must be the case that a physical object is available for appreciation. Recall Vito Acconci's description of *Following Piece* (Figure 1.2): 'Activity, 23 days, varying durations. Choosing a person at random, in the street, any location, each day. Following him wherever he goes, however long or far he travels. (The activity ends when he enters a private place – his home, office, etc.)'. Or Robert Barry's *All the things I know but of which I am not at the moment thinking, 1.36 pm June 15, 1969*. When we're faced with dematerialisation in this sense, we seem to have no *object* to appreciate. As we've seen from Binkley's illuminating discussion of *LHOOQ*, it would be an error to think that the *object* of appreciation is the photographs of the activity of following someone (as if it were a work of photography), or, in the Barry example, the words themselves, written on a wall in New York City (as if it were a work of calligraphy). The photos and the words written on the wall are the mere means by which we grasp the artist's ideas.

This discussion might lead us to one of two possible alternative views about the dematerialisation of the art object. The first view is a relatively modest one, and the second, which we prefer, is much more radical.

Let's take Acconci's *Following Piece* as illustration. The first view is that *Following Piece* is a performance, and that the work is an instance of performance art. According to this view, the performance is the medium whereby we come to appreciate the work. So if this were true, then the precise way the performance is performed matters in our artistic appreciation of the work, just as it matters how Frank Peter Zimmermann performs Beethoven's Violin Concerto in D Major in our appreciation of that work, or how Agnes Oaks performs her role as prima ballerina in *Manon*. But does this really matter with *Following Piece*? Would it make any difference to our artistic appreciation of the work if the performance had been performed in some other way? This seems unlikely, to say the least. Whereas we are influenced by the most subtle of changes to the way the Beethoven is played or the way the dance movements are performed in *Manon*. This view of *Following Piece* is supported by the fact that we have so little to go on in our appreciation of this performance: there is no evidence of the performance itself apart from a few photographs, and these were, as we've already seen, staged at some later time, after the performance was over.[57]

The second view is that *Following Piece* is an instance of conceptual art (not of performance art), and the performance is not the medium, but the mere means by which we come to appreciate the work. If this were true, then the precise way the performance is performed matters no more to our artistic appreciation than does the precise way the goatee beard is drawn in Duchamp's LHOOQ (or the precise way the words are written in the Japanese poem). Recall Sol LeWitt's remark that 'the execution is a perfunctory affair'. Indeed, on this view, it wouldn't matter if the performance didn't take place at all: 'the piece may not be built', in the words of Lawrence Weiner that so infuriated Tom Wolfe. What matters is the idea.

So a lesson from this example (as from the example of the Japanese poem) is that it makes a difference in determining how we are to go about appreciating an artwork what *kind* of artwork it is. In particular the kind of artwork it is will determine (among other things) what is the artistic medium and what is the mere means by which the artistic statement is made.

Other performances by the same artist, Acconci, might be performance art and not conceptual art. For example, Acconci's *Adaptation Studies* consists of three performances by the artist which took place in 1970, and which were filmed in Super 8 by an accomplice.[58] The first, 'Blindfolded Catching', involved a performance of Acconci blindfolded and trying to fend off rubber balls which were being thrown at him. In the second, 'Soap and Eyes', Acconci threw a bowl of soapy water onto his own face and tried to keep his eyes open, making a 'clown's face' in the process. And in the third, 'Hand and Mouth', Acconci tried to make himself sick by forcing his fingers down his throat. Arguably in respect of these works, it is right to appreciate them as performance works and not as conceptual art.

It is controversial how to interpret these works of Acconci, but the point for our purposes is this: if a work is a piece of conceptual art, *then* its artistic appreciation as an artwork will draw just on the ideas as medium, and whatever there is that is physical is mere means: 'the execution is a perfunctory affair'. And in precisely this respect the contrast between Dunchamp's *Fountain* and Botticelli's *Birth of Venus* is very stark: one would be as much in error to focus on the perceptible qualities of the urinal in appreciation of *Fountain* as one would be in error not to focus on the perceptual qualities of the oils on the canvas in appreciation of *Birth of Venus*.

WHERE WE'VE BEEN AND WHERE WE'RE GOING

This chapter has raised more questions than it has answered, and perhaps sewn even more doubts and fears than we started off with. By focusing on how we should engage with and appreciate conceptual art appropriately, we have opened up a Pandora's Box of difficulties ranging from the inadequacy of the object model, to the dematerialisation of the artwork, to the distinction between the medium and the mere means by which an artistic statement is made.

In the next two chapters, we will turn to what has so far mostly been in the background: conceptual art and the aesthetic. In this discussion, we will consider whether the idea idea, involving the thought that conceptual art has no physical medium, can be reconciled with our traditional notion of the aesthetic. In particular, we will ask this question: Is conceptual art really as anti-aesthetic as it sets itself out to be?

Aesthetics and Beyond

Four

INTRODUCTION

In this chapter we set out to explore in more detail what we mean by the traditional, orthodox notion of the aesthetic, and ask whether the fact – if it is a fact – that conceptual art eschews this orthodoxy is one of the central reasons why one might have fears or doubts about conceptual art. We will then consider three possible approaches to conceptual art and the aesthetic. Very roughly, the first approach, *Contra Aesthetics*, endorses conceptual art's claims about the rejection of the aesthetic along the lines we discussed in Chapter three. The second approach, *Aesthetic Traditionalism*, also accepts conceptual art's claims about the rejection of the aesthetic, but holds that this brings into question whether conceptual art really is art, and, even if it is art, whether it really is of any significant artistic value. The third approach, *Aesthetic Idealism*, asks whether conceptual art really does *wholeheartedly* reject the aesthetic as it claims to do. According to this approach, and in spite of its claims, it is possible to ascribe aesthetic value to conceptual art.

To our mind, each of these approaches can be backed up by good arguments. Perhaps, as is often the case in philosophy, there isn't a knockout (or even a knockdown) argument in favour of one particular possibility, and in the end we might be left with a simple choice. What choice we make here will play a big role in our responses to conceptual art: not only in the *way we go about* evaluating it, but also in what value we attach to it when all the cards are on the table. Perhaps it will turn out to be something of a *temperamental choice* – a choice grounded in one's character and personality; but this is to anticipate what we'll say in Chapter five. Let's begin by examining what we usually have in mind when we talk about the aesthetic.

WHAT DOES IT MEAN FOR CONCEPTUAL ART TO BE 'ANTI-AESTHETIC'?

So far we don't yet have a clear idea of what the aesthetic is other than that it's got something to do with perceptual *appearances* – with how the artwork strikes us perceptually. All we've really said is that conceptual art is anti-aesthetic in the sense that it isn't concerned with appearances, and that the perceptual requirement doesn't seem to hold for conceptual art. But we now need to get a better idea of just what the aesthetic is because whether or not conceptual art *really* is anti-aesthetic will, understandably, turn on how this question is answered.

One approach here would be to start by trying to find a traditional notion of the aesthetic that can readily accommodate conceptual art, but this, we believe, would not be faithful to what conceptual artists say and do. For, as we have seen in Chapter one, conceptual artists seem not just indifferent to whether or not conceptual art has aesthetic character, and is thus an appropriate object of aesthetic experience; they seem to set themselves, and their work, firmly and adamantly against it. This is what Binkley had latched onto in his discussion of LHOOQ, and what Duchamp meant when he said that his choice of readymades was 'never dictated by an aesthetic delectation'.[59] So we think the right approach is to begin by examining just what the traditional notion is of the aesthetic, as it is this notion against which conceptual artists are reacting.

Moreover, we think that it's this traditional notion (whatever exactly it turns out to be), which is embedded in our commonsense thinking about art. So the reaction that many of us have to conceptual art – feeling threatened by it, disgusted by it, or even just plain seeing nothing in it – might find its source in this simple idea: when we experience art we hope to have an *aesthetic* experience, and if we have no such experience then we are disappointed, our hopes are frustrated. This might be so even if we can, so to speak, get our heads around the challenges that conceptual art present to the traditional definition, ontology and epistemology of conceptual art. Perhaps this question of the aesthetic is at the very heart of why we have these doubts and fears of conceptual art. So let's now look at what the traditional notion of the aesthetic is. Saying just what it is will turn out to be no easy matter.

THE TRADITIONAL NOTION OF THE AESTHETIC

As with most terms and notions that we frequently use but rarely pause to actually think about (such as consciousness), the notion of the aesthetic tends to conjure up images and associations of the world and its contents that we only have a relatively imprecise grasp of. The first thing that comes to mind when one hears the term 'aesthetic' is most probably of something beautiful, or of an experience of something that is rewarding in much the same way that beautiful things are. The link with art is clearly not very far-fetched, for surely most art sets out to do precisely that, namely to give rise to experiences of beauty (or experiences that bear a strong resemblance to such experiences).

The second thing that comes to mind when thinking or talking about the aesthetic is often a particular artwork, or our experience of that particular work. In this vein, we may reflect on the wonderful feeling that listening to Beethoven's last piano sonatas arouses or the serene sense of harmony that fills us when we admire Canova's sculptures. The traditional notion of the aesthetic, whilst a little vague perhaps, builds this kind of experience into the very heart of its meaning: anything with aesthetic character in this sense is a candidate for being an object of aesthetic appreciation.

To say that something has aesthetic character is generally shorthand for saying that that thing has certain aesthetic features, or properties. And although there are many philosophical theories about how to define aesthetic experience – far too many to go into here – nearly all these accounts agree that aesthetic properties are the focus of our aesthetic experiences. Aesthetic properties are what we appeal to when we try to explain why we find Canova's sculpture harmonious, or when we try to get a friend to see it in the same way as we do. Most important perhaps to the notion of aesthetic experience is the idea that we must engage with these aesthetic properties directly.

AESTHETIC PROPERTIES

Now, most of what we have said so far in this chapter echoes what many of us think, at least at a first glance, about aesthetic properties, namely that the ultimate or paradigmatic aesthetic property must be beauty – the property of being beautiful. And this might well be right. After all, when we pursue aesthetic experiences (such as when we go to an art gallery or go for a walk by the lake) what we seek is to encounter something truly beautiful. But we mustn't lose sight of the fact that there are many other aesthetic properties too, such as being elegant, dainty, luminous, gaudy, crude, harmonious, ethereal, garish, gloomy, and brutal. Importantly, aesthetic properties are very heterogeneous, and the more we think about them the more we realise what a great variety there is. Some seem very closely linked to feelings, emotions and moods (e.g. gloominess) whilst others do not (e.g. luminosity), some are clearly terms of appraisal (e.g. harmoniousness) whilst others are not (e.g. crudity), some give us a detailed idea of how a certain thing looks or appears (e.g. garishness), whilst others do not (e.g. elegance).

To be told that something is beautiful has less descriptive content than to be told that it is, for example, dainty. In other words, if something is described as dainty, we have a rough idea of how that thing may look, even if we haven't seen it ourselves. If, in contrast, we are told that something is beautiful, it is much more difficult to imagine how it might look. In an attempt to make sense of this distinction, philosophers call aesthetic properties with less descriptive content *thin* aesthetic properties, whereas those properties that seem to have more descriptive content are referred to as *thick*.[60] Beauty, it is generally agreed, is a *thin* aesthetic property whilst dainty is *thick*.

In addition, many philosophers would agree that there is a relationship of *dependence* between thin and thick aesthetic properties which works, roughly, like this: something has a thin aesthetic property (e.g. being beautiful) because, or in virtue of, its having certain thicker aesthetic properties (e.g. being dynamic and well-balanced). So a picture is beautiful *because* it is dynamic and well-balanced, and its being beautiful *depends on* its having these thicker aesthetic properties, along with other thick non-aesthetic properties such as being square or being red. Let's call the thicker properties on which the thin aesthetic properties depend the work's *dependence base*.

This may all seem rather abstruse, but in fact it ties in very well with our everyday commonsense thinking about the aesthetic. Consider first the artist and then the audience. The artist, when she sets out to make an artwork, doesn't aim to make something beautiful *just like that*. Rather, she chooses her materials and sets out to work them in a certain way so that the end product, the picture, will have certain thick aesthetic properties in virtue of which it will then be beautiful. Or, putting the point another way, she doesn't, when she has done all her work on the picture, *then* have to do something more to make it beautiful.[61]

Consider next the audience. If we think that a picture we are looking at is beautiful, then we ought to think that there are *reasons* why it is beautiful, and these reasons can be given by appealing to the thicker aesthetic properties which are part of the work's dependence base: it's beautiful *because* it's dynamic and well-balanced, and so on. Of course sometimes we might not be able to put our finger on just what the reasons are ('it just *feels* right' we might say), but with a little time and concentration, we can nearly always come closer to an explanation of why we deem a certain thing beautiful (or not).

Does any of this rather abstract discussion lead us any closer to what it is that makes a property aesthetic? What we need to do, following Binkley's lead, is to find a way to distinguish *aesthetic* properties from a wider category of *artistic* properties. We need to do this, remember, to see how conceptual art such as *LHOOQ* or Robert Barry's *All the things I know* might end up having artistic properties but *not* aesthetic properties. Putting the point in a nutshell, we have still not said what the aesthetic is: all we have is some examples of aesthetic properties. So let's see if we fare any better when we consider the traditional notion of aesthetic experience. Thinking about aesthetic experience may help us to make more progress in distinguishing it from a wider category of artistic experience, which tracks the wider category of artistic properties.

AESTHETIC EXPERIENCE

What is it like to have an aesthetic experience? What, in other words, is the *phenomenology* of aesthetic experience? To consider the phenomenology of a certain kind of experience is, roughly, to consider what it is like to have the thoughts, feelings and impressions that one is subject to when one undergoes that experience. So, one can consider the phenomenology of depression (which involves, for example, the feeling that everything is flat and worthless), the phenomenology of looking over the edge of a steep cliff (which involves, for example, the feeling of dizziness and the impression of losing one's balance), the phenomenology of waking up in the morning, and so on. A satisfactory phenomenology of a kind of experience will be one that anyone who has undergone that kind of experience will, more or less, recognise, and, as they say these days, resonate to. So what we need here is a phenomenology of aesthetic experience, traditionally conceived.

We ask you again to try to remember as well as you can the last experience you had of aesthetic pleasure or delight on looking at a picture – an impressionist or old master perhaps. It is precisely this traditional sense of the aesthetic that conceptual artists are rejecting as any part of their aim. Perhaps you have at some point had the experience of going through an art gallery, moving from, say, the aesthetic delights of the impressionists or the old masters to the room containing conceptual art. No aesthetic pleasure or delight at all! Perhaps you felt disappointed, or even somehow cheated. How can *these things* be art, or have any value, when they fail so miserably (or rather don't even try) to give rise to those delights with which you are so familiar? What's the *point* of it all? Is this why so many people fail to find anything of value in conceptual art, and why so many have doubts and fears about it?

In pursuit of answers to these questions, this chapter will explore the extent to which conceptual art really is anti-aesthetic. Perhaps there is room for aesthetic experience, aesthetic character and aesthetic properties in conceptual art – as long as one is willing to be a little flexible about what is meant by the term 'aesthetic'. To consider this possibility, let's now turn to the relation between conceptual art and the aesthetic, and whether the notion of the aesthetic might in any significant sense be applied to conceptual art.

THREE APPROACHES

We begin by summarising the main claims and assumptions of the three possible approaches raised at the beginning of this chapter.

1 Contra Aesthetics

Aesthetic experience and aesthetic value isn't all that there is to art, or even good art. The ideas that conceptual art evokes are *artistic* ideas, which have artistic value of a kind that doesn't depend on aesthetic value. In contrast, traditional art sets out to have *aesthetic* value as part of its artistic value. Generally, this way of thinking of conceptual art is in line with what many conceptual artists believe they're doing, and it reveals conceptual art as making a fundamental break with traditional conceptions of the aesthetic and with traditional ideas of what makes art good art.

2 Aesthetic Traditionalism
The proper function of art is to provide aesthetic experience, paradigmatically pleasure, in virtue of perceptual encounters with the aesthetic properties of artworks. Conceptual art doesn't provide this kind of experience, but this doesn't necessarily disprove Aesthetic Traditionalism, as Contra Aesthetics claims. Instead, it shows that conceptual art is an 'outlier' to art, and that it isn't really an interesting counterexample to Aesthetic Traditionalism. Generally, we shouldn't take conceptual art as a serious threat to the traditional way in which we think about and value art; it's a tiny blip on the vast landscape of art.

3 Aesthetic idealism
Conceptual art claims to eschew aesthetic properties and aesthetic experience. But we should take with a pinch of salt what conceptual artists say about conceptual art being anti-aesthetic. Instead, and in spite of its manifestos, conceptual art does after all yield a kind of aesthetic experience. It does this through our imaginative engagement with the ideas that are the medium of conceptual art – *aesthetic* ideas. These ideas can have artistic value beyond aesthetic value, but they have that artistic value partly because of the aesthetic value of the ideas that are presented. Thus the break with the traditional idea of art isn't as fundamental as Contra Aesthetics claims, even though Aesthetic Idealism does reject the traditional conception of the aesthetic.

As we progress in our discussion here, we'll see that this debate has significant repercussions for the main topic of Chapter five where we'll be discussing one very important aspect of the artistic value of conceptual art that extends beyond its aesthetic value – if indeed it has any. This is the *cognitive value* of conceptual art, or the contribution that conceptual art can make to our knowledge. But now let's turn to our first approach to conceptual art and aesthetics.

CONTRA AESTHETICS

We already know that, according to the traditional conception, aesthetic character and value is closely linked to beauty, aesthetic pleasure and a restricted understanding of the reward we stand to gain from engaging with aesthetic properties. We also know that this is precisely the kind of experience that conceptual art rejects as fundamental to our experience of art. This rejection is manifested in the approach of conceptual artists in a number of related ways. First, there is the dematerialisation of the artwork that we first encountered in Chapter one. As we saw there, a work such as Vito Acconci's *Following Piece* (Figure 1.2) doesn't seem to provide us with a physical thing or a performance which can be a suitable object of aesthetic appreciation in the traditional sense. The performance itself was an event, and the photographic record of the event was physical, but we don't look for *beauty* in the performance or in the photos, and if we were to try to find it there, we'd be making some kind of mistake.

Second, even if there is a physical thing which has what might be thought to be aesthetic properties (even being beautiful perhaps) – such as the urinal that Duchamp presented – its choice by the artist was, in Duchamp's own words from Chapter one, 'never dictated by an aesthetic delectation'. The physical thing is *merely the means* by which the idea is presented to us.

Third, in its rejection of the perceptual requirement, refusing to provide us with aesthetic delectation from the presentation of perceptible aesthetic features, conceptual art chooses to offer us something else. Instead of aesthetic interest, it aims, to use Duchamp's words again, 'towards other regions more verbal' – towards ideas. And this is precisely where conceptual art leads us, away from the aesthetic and towards the *idea idea*. It's nicely summed up by these remarks of the art critic Roberta Smith:

> Conceptual activity was united by an almost unanimous emphasis on language or on linguistically analogous systems, and by a conviction [. . .] that language and ideas were the true essence of art, that *visual experience and sensory delectation were secondary and inessential*, if not downright mindless and immoral.[62]

Accordingly, most conceptual art is anti-aesthetic in a more profound way than simply not aiming for beauty. The Dadaists were anti-aesthetic in this less profound sense. For example, the Dadaists Max Ernst and Otto Dix, as well as the German expressionist Max Beckmann, portrayed the horrors of the First World War and its aftermath in Berlin – mutilation, torture, rape – with a shocking and ruthless directness of gaze that is, even now, hard to look at. Arthur Danto in his piece '*Kalliphobia* [meaning hatred of beauty] in Contemporary Art' reports Ernst as saying 'My works of that period were not meant to attract, but to make people scream', and another Dadaist George Grosz said 'I drew and painted out of a spirit of contradiction, trying in my works to convince the world that it was ugly, sick, and mendacious'.[63] So what the Dadaists were rejecting, in their intentional portrayal of the world's ugliness, and of man's unredeeming brutality to man, was *beauty* rather than aesthetics. For ugliness is, we mustn't forget, an aesthetic property. And the ugliness of the Dadaist pictures and drawings is a *perceptible* aesthetic property. Conceptual art's rejection of the aesthetic is a rejection of the whole notion, rather than just of positive aesthetic properties such as beauty.

So, if we adhere to the approach promoted by Contra Aesthetics, aesthetic properties aren't necessary for something to qualify as art: art can get on perfectly well without them. This, we think, is a correct interpretation of what we might call the *manifesto* of conceptual art. (Talk of manifestos suggests that conceptual art is a more cohesive movement than it actually is, so we should use that term with this warning in mind.)

But conceptual art, at least in its purest form, goes further than this. This purest form was perhaps most evident in the 1960s, in for example work by Robert Barry such as *Inert Gas: Helium* (Figure 2.3) and *All the things I know*. In this purest form conceptual art seems not only to hold that aesthetic properties aren't necessary for art, but also that aesthetic properties, and even any physical presence at all, *get in the way of* art: they get in the way of other, more important, kinds of artistic value. That is to say, we're better off without aesthetic properties, and without anything physical.

Why might one think this? Why claim that art is better off without the aesthetic? (We ask this question with the warning about manifestos in mind.) The answer is that it may detract from what really matters in art, namely the idea or the thought 'behind' the art, so to speak. If we are to focus our appreciation on the idea, we need to abstract entirely from the physical thing, from everything material. What is left is, then, a *purely intellectual process of art-making* and, correspondingly, a *purely intellectual process of art appreciation*.

An analogy might help here. Sometimes television news has to deal with something quite complex, which requires an intellectual grasp of abstract concepts. For example, the increase in the money supply that has just been reported by the central monetary authority might have serious implications for the economy. Being a visual medium, the producers of the television news feel they need to show us some images, so they might, for example, show us a film of coins or notes of currency coming off the central bank's production line, or shoppers handing over money in a supermarket. Having these images in front of us often does have the effect of getting in the way of our grasp of what really matters here. We would be better off if we didn't have to see these *pictures* of money, for we find ourselves having distracting thoughts – for example, wondering what the particular shopper is buying, or being impressed by the speed and efficiency of the production line. What really matters is the money supply, and this idea, from macro-economics, is not a visual notion at all. One might put it like this, turning Marshall McLuhan's famous saying on its head: *the medium isn't the message; the medium gets in the way of the message*.

Now let's apply the analogy to conceptual art. Acconci's *Following Piece* (Figure 1.2) says a lot of interesting things about privacy in a public space, and what it is to be intruded on. Remember the words: 'Activity, 23 days, varying durations. Choosing a person at random, in the street, any location, each day. Following him wherever he goes, however long or far he travels. (The activity ends when he enters a private place – his home, office, etc.)'. But in addition to the words, we are presented with some grainy pictures, and these, like the images of money on our TV screens, do tend to distract from our intellectual engagement with what is at the heart of this work: perhaps we find ourselves curious about the 1960s clothes worn by the participants, or wondering in which part of which city the events took place.

In contrast, Robert Barry's *All the things I know* is purer, just in the sense that *all we have* that is physical are the words written on the wall: no images to get in the way of our proper intellectual appreciation of the work. The medium doesn't get in the way of the message. Or, more precisely but a *lot* less snappily, and remembering our distinction between medium and mere means: the physical means doesn't get in the way of the idea which is the medium by which the message is communicated.

We're very sympathetic to this emphasis on the intellectual aspect of the appreciation of conceptual art. We are often better placed to appreciate a work of conceptual art without a physical presence to distract us. But we aren't convinced that the dematerialisation of the artwork need be at the expense of the aesthetic altogether. Nor are we convinced that conceptual art, understood in this way, clearly does enough to distinguish itself from other intellectual pursuits which focus on ideas – philosophy for example. These issues will arise again in our discussion of Aesthetic Idealism. Before we get there, though, we need to consider something much more familiar and . . . traditional, namely Aesthetic Traditionalism.

AESTHETIC TRADITIONALISM

Aesthetic Traditionalism brings us back to our discussion of definition in Chapter two, where we briefly explored the notion of a functional definition of art. Aesthetic Traditionalism is, quite clearly, directed towards precisely such a definition for, according to aesthetic traditionalists, giving rise to aesthetic experience is nothing other than the proper function of art. Aesthetic Traditionalism urges us to look at art as it has been through the centuries, not just in the Western world, but elsewhere too. Wherever we look over this vast historical landscape, traditionalists say, we will find that our practices of art making and art appreciation aim at the creation and appreciation of works that give rise to a special kind of pleasure – aesthetic pleasure.

There's no doubt that aesthetic experience is a real phenomenon in our lives, and it's a very important part of what it is to live well. Imagine what a bleak life it would be without such experience – a dystopian world where there are no aesthetic properties and thus no possibility of aesthetic experience. Of course this isn't to suggest that aesthetic experience was only possible at the time when production of the 'fine arts' was underway in the seventeenth century, at the time when creation of objects purely for aesthetic pleasure was the activity of those people we call 'artists'. On the contrary, the idea is that this kind of pleasure was available in just the same way to a thirteenth century traveller to Paris on seeing Notre Dame for the first time, or to a Homeric warrior on seeing a finely-wrought shield, or to a Chinese peasant at the time of the Ming dynasty on seeing a beautifully painted screen door.

These last three examples show another thing about Aesthetic Traditionalism. It doesn't hold that aesthetic appreciation is the *only* purpose of making these objects. There is plenty of room in Aesthetic Traditionalism for things made for other purposes – quilts, pots, houses, cathedrals, shields, screen doors, chairs, scrolls, and so on – just so long as a significant *part* of their creation was for aesthetic purposes. We can then readily contrast the chair made simply and solely for the purpose of sitting on, and the chair made for that purpose *and* for the purpose of giving rise to aesthetic pleasure.

But Aesthetic Traditionalism faces three real challenges.[64] The first is whether it really has the nerve to reject all or most of conceptual art as art on the grounds that it doesn't have the required aesthetic character. For, surely, to do this is to fly in the face of the informed opinion of the art world of today. The second challenge is that not only conceptual art and much other modern art but also an enormous amount of great traditional art seeks to give rise to experiences which aren't aesthetic in the rather limited sense being used by the aesthetic traditionalist, but which are still, in the wider sense, aesthetic. The third challenge is that Aesthetic Traditionalism has too narrow an idea of what aesthetic experience is, and of how it arises.

The first challenge is at heart one about definition. Many philosophers take it to be a – or even *the* – central purpose of a definition to come up with something that fits our intuitions about what there is in the world: to include what we intuitively think should be included, and to exclude what we think should be excluded. Recalling our earlier analogy with consciousness, it would (to say the least) count against our definition of consciousness if it implied that plants were conscious, or if it implied that your cat wasn't conscious.[65]

The right response to this challenge on behalf of Aesthetic Traditionalism is, we think, to shift the emphasis of the debate. Let's try a different analogy to see how this might work. Say you were interested in giving a philosophically interesting and worthwhile account of the emotion of shame. The right place to begin with such a project, we suggest, wouldn't be to aim to provide a definition which includes all and only instances of what we would intuitively think of as shame. Much better to think about some central cases of shame and think about what is important in these central cases: the causes and effects of shame, its phenomenology, its morality, the contrast between shame and guilt, the cross-cultural variations in shame, and so on. Doing all this should throw some clear light on the phenomenon, and help us to see important connections which otherwise might not be noticed. If at the end of this project someone were to claim that we have excluded some kind of shame response, we might simply reply that we haven't considered this to be a central case, and that we are happy to remain neutral as to whether it is really shame or not.

The analogous response for the aesthetic traditionalist is to say that the central cases of art are aesthetic, and that we can learn a lot about the nature and purpose of art making and art appreciation if the aesthetic is our focus. The aesthetic traditionalist can then remain neutral about whether conceptual art really is art or not, keeping the focus clearly on what matters for the explanatory project. Definition really isn't as important as explanation.[66]

This response to the first challenge comes at a cost, although it is a cost that the aesthetic traditionalist is most probably more than willing to bear. The cost is that conceptual art is no longer important when we are thinking about art; it begins to take on the status of an outlier, something of an aberration which doesn't belong to the canon. In contrast, the opponent of Aesthetic Traditionalism will insist that in adopting this approach we are missing something important: not only important in thinking about art, but also important in terms of our possible range of experience of art. Conceptual art, the opponent says, is artistically interesting in ways that the aesthetic traditionalist fails to see.

The second challenge follows up on the first, and centres on the thought that Aesthetic Traditionalism works with too narrow a conception of what matters in art – holding that it is aesthetic properties only that *really* matter. By doing this, Aesthetic Traditionalism excludes not only conceptual art (and *avant garde* art in general), which it is perfectly happy to do. It also excludes much of *traditional* art. As a result the explanatory project of Aesthetic Traditionalism fails properly to consider what is really important about art *in addition to* aesthetics in the traditional sense. Putting it bluntly, its focus – what it sets out to explain – is too narrow.[67] Let's put some meat on this challenge.

To begin with, we need to think a bit more about the pleasure that we get in our engagement with art. Now, there's no doubt that aesthetic pleasure is an important part of what we experience when we engage with a work of art. But – and this is the heart of this second challenge to Aesthetic Traditionalism – aesthetic pleasure isn't the only kind of experience that we have in our artistic engagement with an artwork. Sometimes these other kinds of artistic experience will arise *in addition to* aesthetic pleasure at the same object; and sometimes they will arise *without* any aesthetic pleasure. But either way, we think, Aesthetic Traditionalism doesn't pay proper regard to these important experiences.

So what might these other kinds of experience and other kinds of properties be? (Remember here that we are looking for *artistic* properties and experiences that aren't aesthetic. We don't want to include the experience of pleasures of ownership, or of sitting in a comfy chair.) First, there is the experience of pleasure that isn't aesthetic pleasure which arises, for example, when one finally grasps the meaning of a work of art (narrative or pictorial or of some other kind), perhaps after a lot of research into its background. This is really a kind of intellectual pleasure. For example, one might gain intellectual pleasure from coming to realise that Stanley Kubrick in his film *Paths of Glory* (1957) was imitating the tracking shots of Max Ophüls.[68] This kind of pleasure will be familiar to you not only from experiencing art, but from elsewhere too: intellectual pleasure such as you experience on working out the solution to a crossword clue, or on finally coming to understand the complex argument in a philosophical work that you have been struggling with. These examples might suggest that intellectual pleasure only arises from finally finding an answer or from finally solving a problem, but we shouldn't forget the pleasure in the intellectual activity itself, prior to finding the solution (just as one can feel pleasure in straining every muscle on a long run – the pleasure isn't only in getting to the destination). Clearly, artworks' being able to provide these kinds of pleasures doesn't in any way depend on their having aesthetic properties.

The second kind of experience that Aesthetic Traditionalism doesn't pay proper regard to is not to do with pleasure at all. In a way, it's even misleading to call it a kind of *experience*. What we have in mind is the gaining of knowledge. This will take centre stage in Chapter five, but the main idea here is that many artworks, including narrative artworks such as novels and biographies, and plays, operas, pictures, sculptures and so on, all have the potential to provide us with valuable knowledge. Artworks that provide this knowledge, we'll be arguing, have cognitive value (roughly, they have value *because* they provide valuable knowledge), and this cognitive value is an important part of many works' artistic value over and above any aesthetic value that they have.

The third challenge to Aesthetic Traditionalism quickly leads us to Aesthetic Idealism, so we can be brief with it here. The central thought is that an artwork's *ideas* can have a certain kind of aesthetic value, and that this value is different from that which Aesthetic Traditionalism concentrates on. More specifically, these artworks don't depend on *perceptual* experience to be a source of enjoyment.

To sum up these last two challenges to Aesthetic Traditionalism, then, we think that it is highly questionable to claim that any art that doesn't have at its heart *aesthetic* experience through *perceptual* engagement with an artwork's aesthetic properties in the traditional sense is 'a miniscule phenomenon', as Nick Zangwill puts it.[69] Much art sets out to provide, and succeeds in providing, experiences that are not aesthetic in this traditional sense.

AESTHETIC IDEALISM

As we've seen, both Contra Aesthetics and Aesthetic Traditionalism accept that conceptual art succeeds in its rejection of the aesthetic, although, of course, they draw very different conclusions from this. Aesthetic Idealism opens up a third possibility, by questioning whether conceptual art really does succeed in its rejection of the aesthetic – or at least whether its success is as complete as might be supposed. How does it go about this?

Before addressing this concern, let's first eliminate another way of questioning the success of conceptual art in its rejection of the aesthetic. This would be to insist that conceptual artworks are, after all, aesthetic *in the traditional sense of that term*. Consider again Duchamp's *Fountain* (Figure 1.3). This way of questioning the success of conceptual art's rejection of the aesthetic is simply to point towards the urinal's highly perceptible properties, which do seem to be aesthetic in the traditional sense (the sheen of the porcelain, the smoothness of the lines, and so on), and hold that *Fountain* is beautiful rather in the way that *Mona Lisa* is.

We think this is a hopeless strategy. First, any perceptible aesthetic properties of this kind that *Fountain* has will be shared by other urinals from the same warehouse, so they can't be artistic properties; they might as well be *plumbing* properties.[70] And secondly, it's quite clear that many of the works of conceptual art that we have been considering don't have any perceptible properties that could possibly be considered to be of the kind that could give rise to aesthetic pleasure. Consider once more *Following Piece* (Figure 1.2), or Joseph Kosuth's *One and Three Chairs* (Figure 1.4) or Robert Barry's *Inert Gas: Helium* (Figure 2.3). One would look in vain for traditional aesthetic properties in these works.

Furthermore, if one were to allow the aesthetic into conceptual art in the traditional sense, there's a serious danger that one would go about appreciating conceptual art in the wrong way: looking for perceptible aesthetic properties in the traditional sense, and then either being disappointed when there are none (*Following Piece*), or being pleased when they are present, and thus appreciating the work in the wrong way (*Fountain*). We say 'the wrong way' because, as we've already seen, what is perceptually present to us in conceptual art is not the artistic medium, and is not part of what one ought to focus on in appreciation; the real value of conceptual art lies elsewhere, as we'll see in Chapter five.

A caveat is needed here: much *avant garde* art which isn't conceptual art, but which in some sense owes its existence to that movement, does aim to give rise to aesthetic pleasure. We have in mind, for example, many of the works of Jeff Koons and Olafur Eliasson, such as *Balloon Dog* and *The Weather Project*. By no means is all *avant garde* art anti-aesthetic.

What, then, is Aesthetic Idealism?[71] Its essential strategy is to return to the idea idea, and to develop the thought that *ideas can have aesthetic properties*. Aesthetic Idealism can accept the idea idea, and endorse the rejection of anything physical (whether object or performance) as part of the artistic medium, whilst still questioning whether these tenets need imply a ban on aesthetic character. In other words, it sets out to make room for aesthetic appreciation, even though not the traditional kind of aesthetic appreciation that most conceptual artists reject. The thought driving Aesthetic Idealism is something like this: if the conceptual artwork is dematerialised and the artistic medium is the idea itself, then conceptual art is only truly and absolutely anti-aesthetic if there is no room for ideas to have aesthetic value. So, can ideas have aesthetic properties?

Let's consider how this might work outside conceptual art, and outside art in general. What we need to do is first to distinguish between perceptible properties and what we will call *experiential* properties. Perceptible properties are those properties that can be perceived. Experiential properties are those that can be experienced. What can be experienced is a broader category than what can be perceived. Redness, for example, is a perceptible property (you can see it), and is thus an experiential property (in seeing it you can experience it). In contrast, wittiness isn't a perceptible property (you can't see it or otherwise perceive it), but it is nevertheless an experiential property (you can experience it without perceiving it). You might comment here that you do need to perceive *something* in order to experience the wittiness of a joke: you need to see the words on the page, or hear the words spoken, or see the gesture made. Agreed, but the words on the page, the spoken words, the gesture, aren't themselves what is witty, they are merely the means by which the wittiness of the joke is communicated in order to be experienced. You can hear the words, and understand their meaning, but not 'get' the joke.

Could the aesthetic properties of ideas be rather like those of wittiness: experiential but not perceptible? (Remember that the traditional notion of the aesthetic ties aesthetic properties to perception, so this is where the break with traditional aesthetics begins – a bigger break than Dadaism.) To begin with the thicker aesthetic properties, we can readily think of examples of these from outside art: examples where something has a thick non-perceptible but experiential aesthetic property. A mathematical proof's *elegance* would be one such, or the *crudeness* of a refutation of a philosophical argument. Moving from the thick to the thin, the mathematical proof might also be *beautiful* because of its elegance, or the philosophical argument *ugly* because of its crudeness. And in our moral discourse, we find many such aesthetic terms which aren't perceptual in the traditional sense, as the philosopher Colin McGinn has pointed out: 'There are many terms of this type: for example, on the positive side, "fine", "pure", "stainless", "sweet", "wonderful"; and on the negative side (which is richer), "rotten", "vile", "foul", "ugly", "sick", "repulsive", "tarnished"'.[72] Thus someone's character can be tarnished, a generous action fine, a thought vile, a passion repulsive.

But these examples from outside art might give rise to an immediate and serious challenge. Aren't these aesthetic terms, thick and thin, being used in a *metaphorical* sense? Surely, ideas, character traits, and passions aren't *literally* beautiful? This complaint can't just be dismissed out of hand, although it's not obvious how one would settle the dispute.

One thing to be borne in mind here is just how far our aesthetic talk extends outside the domain of art (and of nature): beautiful ideas and character traits; football as the beautiful game; elegant ways of dressing and of entering a room; ugly phrases; tarnished political programmes. How can we draw a line here, without being so restrictive as to limit aesthetic properties only to what is perceptible; or at the other extreme, without being so open as to allow anything at all at least potentially to have an aesthetic property?

A complete answer to the question would take up much more space than we have here; the role of metaphor in our discourse is a much-disputed philosophical topic.[73] But let's look at another example which we hope will go some way to dissolving the force of the question: to dissolving the thought that we have to find a clear dividing-line between what is literal and what is metaphorical (and perhaps also between what is perceptible and what is experiential but not perceptible). City financiers, in particular those who seem to attach more importance to lining their own pockets than to benefiting their shareholders, are often referred to as *fat cats*. (Note that this is a metaphor: it's not suggesting that city financiers are like, or analogous to, fat cats.) What the image conjures up – for it does conjure an image – is wholly appropriate to its object: the fat feline, lying in the sun purring, and not moving itself unless there's some cream in the offing. And this is just how city financiers are often portrayed in newspaper cartoons: sometime even cigar-smoking like the cat in Bulgakov's *Master and Marguerita*. In calling them fat cats, it would be silly to say that they are *literally* fat cats. But the fact that it would be silly to say this doesn't imply that the use of the term is *merely* metaphorical. What, after all is a *mere* metaphor? For thinking of them as fat cats does affect how we think of them. It *colours* (another metaphor) our perception of them: there is a sense in which we *see* and *hear* them purring self-contentedly, licking their lips, with the kind of enigmatic smile that cats have.

A similar kind of response can be given to how we apply aesthetic properties to states of character and to ideas. Thinking of someone's character as tarnished or ugly colours our perception of them. (It's for this reason that we find it so shocking that someone has that kind of bad character and yet they appear, like Oscar Wilde's eponymous Dorian Gray, to be perfectly lovely.) Here too it's a mistake to say that someone's character is *literally* tarnished, just as it is to say that this city financier is *literally* purring; but we can also see here too why it would be wrong to say that it's *merely* a metaphor when the use of a metaphor can so much influence our way of thinking about, and of perceiving, the target of the metaphor.

So let's accept that ideas can have aesthetic properties which aren't immediately perceptible properties. If this is right, ideas can be *aesthetically* valuable because of the kind of *aesthetic* experience that they provide. For example, when we look at Duchamp's *Fountain* (Figure 1.3), the pleasure we feel isn't (or at least it shouldn't be) pleasure at the perceptible aesthetic properties of the urinal – the sheen of the porcelain and so on. Instead, the pleasure is at the sheer *ingenuity* (and *cheek* perhaps) of the idea that Duchamp had, and that he realised in this way – as a means to bringing before the world the whole question of what can be art. With Joseph Kosuth's *One and Three Chairs* (Figure 1.4), the aesthetic pleasure is at the *elegance* of Kosuth's idea of representing a certain complex philosophical problem, distilling complex relationships into an apparently simple juxtaposition. And finally, Michael Craig-Martin's *An Oak Tree* (Figure 4.1) presents a complex theological issue with great *subtlety*.

We'll return to the philosophical and theological issues that Kosuth and Craig-Martin raise in their pieces in Chapter five, and to the whole question of the cognitive value of conceptual art – the value that conceptual art has in virtue of the knowledge that it communicates. The point for now, though, is the relation between the cognitive value of conceptual art

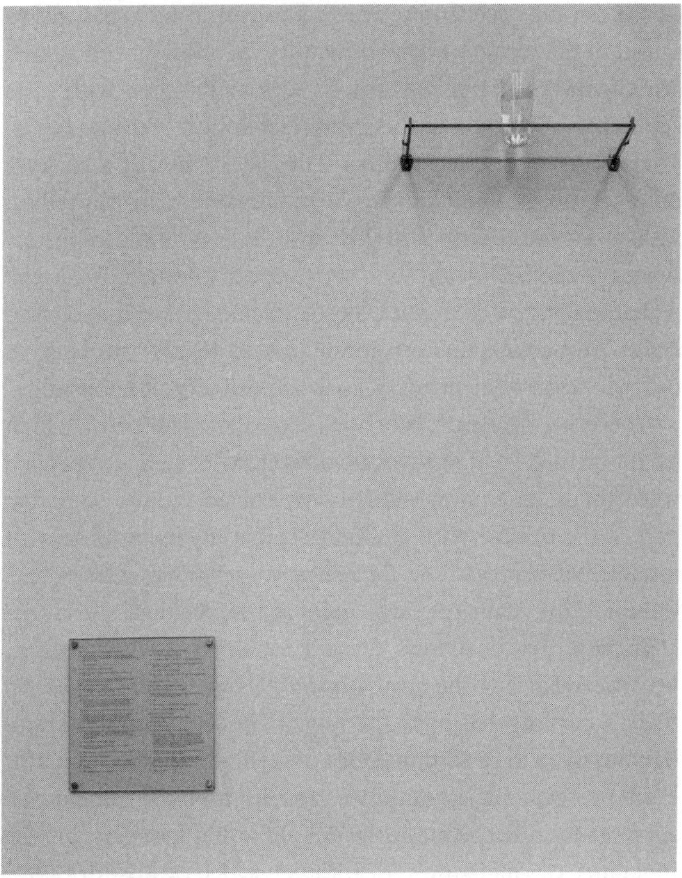

Figure 4.1 Michael Craig-Martin, *An Oak Tree*.

and its aesthetic value. Aesthetic Idealism holds that the aesthetic properties of ideas in conceptual art can be valuable not only in their own right, valuable aesthetically, but that they can also be valuable because of the way in which they enable knowledge to be communicated.

We can now see that Aesthetic Idealism in no way seeks to question the idea idea or to downplay the value of conceptual art. On the contrary. Nor does it seek to disagree with conceptual art's rejection of the traditional notion of the aesthetic. The notion Aesthetic Idealism relies on is instead a broader one that can be applied to artworks fundamentally centred on ideas – artworks with a highly unorthodox ontology. In this sense, then, being anti-aesthetic doesn't follow from the dematerialisation of the art object as conceptual artists so often claim. And conceptual art doesn't *need* to be anti-aesthetic in order to achieve its primary goal: the delivery of knowledge.

There is one final challenge to Aesthetic Idealism which might be made by the advocate of Contra Aesthetics. When we were discussing Contra Aesthetics we considered the claim that part of the trouble with aesthetics is that it gets in the way of intellectual appreciation: *the medium gets in the way of the message*. Couldn't this challenge be brought against Aesthetic Idealism?

In fact, this challenge doesn't touch Aesthetic Idealism, because what has the aesthetic properties is *the idea itself*. So there is nothing getting in the way of intellectual appreciation. In contrast to the traditional idea of aesthetic appreciation, this kind of aesthetic appreciation results *from* the intellectual appreciation – for example the delight results *from* grasping the ingenuity of Duchamp's idea, the elegance of Kosuth's idea, the subtlety of Craig-Martin's idea.

WHERE WE'VE BEEN AND WHERE WE'RE GOING

This discussion of our three possible approaches to conceptual art and the aesthetic – Contra Aesthetics, Aesthetic Traditionalism, and Aesthetic Idealism – might have masked one essential point on which all three agree. This point is that conceptual art *doesn't provide us with aesthetic experience in the traditional sense*. The differences between the three approaches amount to how one is to respond to this: by saying that art without aesthetics is fine; by saying that art without aesthetics is an uninteresting outlier; or by saying that art without aesthetics in the traditional sense is fine, but that there is still room for the possibility that ideas can have aesthetic properties.

Nevertheless, we *are* left with a significant absence in conceptual art: an absence that is so readily filled by our perceptual encounters with so much traditional art – whether by presenting us with the beautiful to delight us, or with the ugly to shock and horrify us.

As we'll see in Chapter five, traditional aesthetic pleasure isn't the only significant absence. For there are other ways in which we engage with traditional art that aren't available to us in many (not all) works of conceptual art: we have in mind in particular *emotional involvement*. So what we will have to do in Chapter five is to consider whether our engagement with conceptual art can still be a worthwhile experience for us in spite of these significant absences. What we will find is that the cognitive or intellectual value of conceptual art will have a lot of work to do to fill in these absences. And then the question will be whether cognitive value is up to this task. One answer might be that it is for some of us, but not for all of us. Perhaps, after all, it will turn out that conceptual art isn't for everyone.

What's Left Once Aesthetic Appreciation Has Gone?

Five

INTRODUCTION

Let's remember once more our theme: the way we should go about evaluating conceptual art, and more widely the way we should think about it, depends on prior answers to questions about definition, ontology, epistemology and aesthetics. What we've found so far is that in many important respects, the break that conceptual art has made with traditional art is a substantial one. Conceptual art challenges the traditional notion of the definition of art (when it's understood as fulfilling some kind of function), of the ontology of art (understood as encapsulated in the object model), and of the epistemology of art (understood as expressed in terms of the perceptual requirement). But what we think is the most significant break of all, the one that most affects our responses to conceptual art, is the idea idea and the resulting rejection of the traditional notion of the aesthetic. Remember that conceptual art is anti-aesthetic not just in the sense that it rejects the idea that we appreciate the beauty of artworks; it rejects the very idea that art should involve any physical things (whether objects or performances) with any immediately perceptible aesthetic properties at all. And in rejecting ugliness just as much as it rejects beauty, it represents a much more momentous break with traditional art than German expressionism, which set out in its art to show the ugliness of the world in unalloyed form.

This rejection of the aesthetic is the most significant break of all, we think, because the aesthetic is at the heart of much of our engagement with, and appreciation of, traditional art. Again, we ask you to think of how you appreciate your favourite works of traditional art: paintings – the Vermeer, the Botticelli, the Renoir; sculptures – the Canova, the Brancusi, the Rodin; music – the Beethoven, the Mozart, the Britten; novels – the Tolstoy, the Conrad, the Woolf. Not only do these traditional works of art give us aesthetic experiences of the kind we discussed in Chapters three and four. They also connect in all sorts of ways with our emotions, and they do so often because of what the works represent and the way they represent it. We can go back to these works time and time again without tiring of them, still responding much as we did the first time.

Consider for example, Degas's picture, *The Absinthe Drinker* (Figure 5.1). It shows the desolation of a life given up to alcohol, but more than that, it shows the loneliness that each of us faces in our own particular way. It reveals something profound about the human condition. One cannot help but be moved emotionally in all sorts of ways. It might be a matter of dispute exactly how such emotional responses are part of our aesthetic appreciation of the artwork, but there is no doubt that they seem part and parcel of the experience that we have when we engage with traditional art. The capacity of works such as this to give rise to emotional responses is part of why we value them so highly.

This whole experience, aesthetic and emotional, that we have in engaging with and appreciating these works is missing with conceptual art. And remember that this is part of what conceptual art unashamedly sets out to do: it sets out to be anti-aesthetic, and to engage the mind rather than the heart. So by its own lights this doesn't constitute a failure on its part. Indeed, as we saw in Chapter four, conceptual art in

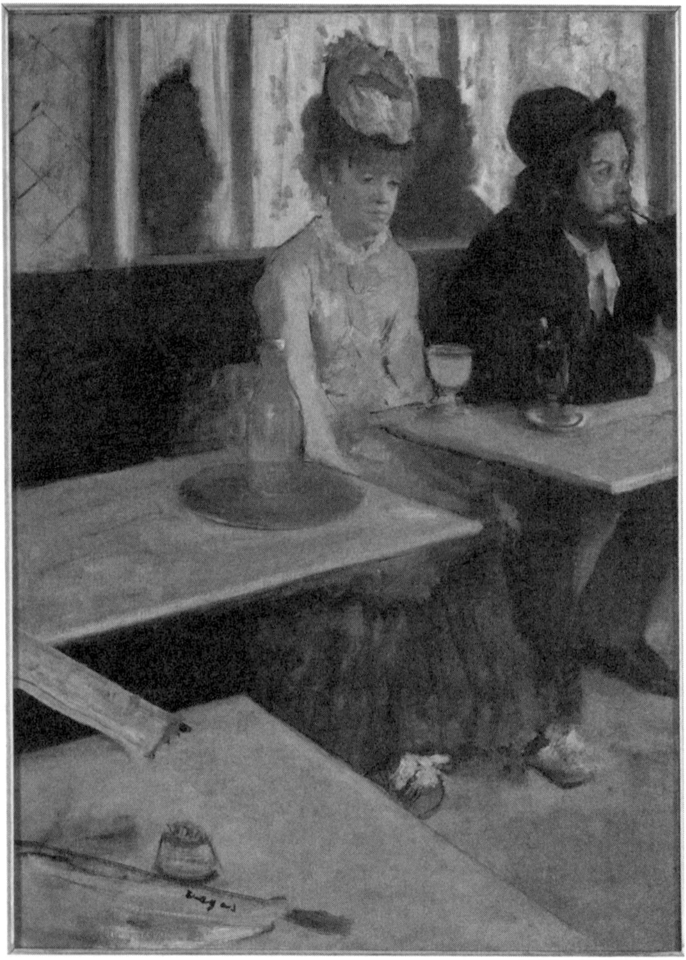

Figure 5.1 Edgar Degas, *l'absinthe*.

photo RMN
Edgar Degas : Dans un café, dit aussi L'absinthe, vers 1875-76 (RF 1984)

Paris, musée d'Orsay, legs du comte Isaac de Camondo

its 'purest' form sees the aesthetic as getting in the way of a proper appreciation of what it has to offer in the place of the aesthetic.

So what does conceptual art have to offer instead? Does what it offers instead make up for what it has so willingly given up? And finally, does what it offers turn art into something so different that it might not even qualify as art? These are the central questions that will preoccupy us in this last chapter. We began to see the answers to some of them in earlier chapters, so we'll pick up the thread from there.

Before that, however, we should make one thing clear. It would be quite wrong to say that conceptual art fails as art simply because it doesn't provide the kind of aesthetic appreciation and emotional engagement that we get from traditional art. That would be to bias things in favour of traditional art before the discussion even gets off the ground. Some of us prefer chocolate sauce on our ice cream, and others don't. But this is just a matter of taste, and it doesn't get us to anything like an objective measure of whether ice cream with chocolate sauce is better than ice cream without. Subjective preference doesn't get us to objective superiority. Nor for that matter does shared subjective preference: most of us might prefer chocolate sauce with our ice cream, and yet ice cream on its own might still be superior. (Think of how English cooking used to be really bad, and yet most English people liked it, preferring their vegetables overcooked rather than *al dente*.) Similarly, if you happen to have a preference for the aesthetic delights of traditional art over whatever conceptual art has to offer in its stead, or even if most of us have this preference, this in no way gets us to the objective superiority of traditional art over conceptual art. (Or the other way around of course: a preference for conceptual art doesn't get you to *its* superiority either.) To get to objective superiority, we need something like a good *argument*.

There is, in fact, an argument available to us that does have some bite, and that might well get us to something more objective than mere preference. We'll turn to it later, but it might be worthwhile to give a hint of it at this stage. The argument will remind us of the functional definition of art: the idea that the purpose of art is to fulfil some kind of human need, although, as we'll see, the point can be made without appeal to any question of definition as such. If it's right that art ought to fulfil a human need, and if that need turns out not to be satisfied by conceptual art, then we'll have something like an objective reason to think that conceptual art really does lack something important, and this might explain why so many of us shy away from it.

INTELLECTUAL INTEREST IN IDEAS

Let's begin, though, with what conceptual art offers us instead of aesthetic pleasure (in the traditional sense). Our suggestion, consistent with Aesthetic Idealism and the idea idea, is that the main thing that it offers is *intellectual* interest and pleasure. By 'intellectual' we mean simply to do with the intellect or with ideas. Someone who is an intellectual is someone who is interested in ideas.[74] So in this sense the term doesn't have any elitist connotation, and it has no necessary connection to intelligence: someone can be intelligent and non-intellectual, and intellectual and not particularly intelligent.

Conceptual art, then, is intellectual just in the sense that it is concerned with ideas, and, in particular, although not exclusively, with *philosophical* ideas. We will broadly classify this concern with philosophical ideas into two groups.

First, there are those pieces that raise philosophical challenges to traditional ideas about art. We have seen this in our discussion from earlier chapters: let's look back at some of them. Duchamp's *Fountain* (Figure 1.3) raises challenges to our traditional definition of art through his action of submitting it to the Society of Independent Artists, which, you will remember, concluded that it was 'by no means a work of art'. Robert Barry's *Inert Gas: Helium* (Figure 2.3) and his *All the things I know but of which I am not at the moment thinking* both challenge our traditional ontology of art through the dematerialisation of the artwork. These two works also challenge our epistemology of art because the perceptual requirement is traduced.

It's the second broad group that we will focus on in this chapter. These are the works of conceptual art that raise philosophical (and other) ideas which are not directly concerned to challenge our traditional ideas *about art*. As we will see, they are still *philosophically knowing* in the reflective sense that we discussed in Chapter one, but they aren't philosophically knowing *about art* in the self-reflective way that the first group is.

PHILOSOPHICALLY KNOWING CONCEPTUAL ART

We already encountered one such philosophically knowing work in Chapter one, namely Rosemarie Trockel's *Cogito ergo sum* (Figure 1.6). You will remember that this work included the words 'cogito ergo sum' machine-knitted onto the woollen fabric, and in this way it raises all sorts of interesting questions about the proof that Descartes used in his *Meditations* to show that he existed. Descartes' very act of thinking 'cogito' or 'I am thinking' enabled him, he argued, to reach the conclusion that he existed as a 'thinking thing' ('une chose qui pense'). In

Chapter one, we said that Trockel's piece was an interesting joke on the 'cogito': the words were machine-knitted, but they were in no way a guarantee that the knitting-machine was a thinking thing, or even that it existed at all.

Trockel's piece is thus philosophically knowing: it demonstrates knowledge of the essentials of Descartes' famous argument. Moreover, it *requires*, if it is to be properly appreciated, a similar degree of knowledge on behalf of the person who engages with the work. (In Chapter one, we also said that the piece was *esoteric* in the sense that the fact that it was machine-knitted, a fact vital to appreciation, wasn't available from inspection of the work itself or of its title. We'll be considering this shortly in relation to the idea that a work such as this is *discourse-dependent*. But for now, let's just assume that we know it was machine-knitted.)

Let's call the person who engages with the work Ann. What has to be true about Ann for her properly to appreciate the piece? First, as we've just seen, it requires a certain amount of philosophical knowledge. But let's assume that Ann doesn't possess such knowledge: all her training has been elsewhere, in the sciences perhaps, and she has never done any philosophy. Now, Ann certainly could make the effort of finding out a few facts about Descartes' argument (perhaps the gallery where it's exhibited has a brief synopsis in the brochure). Still, this might well not be enough to enable her to gain the right appreciative stance. In a way it would be rather like having a joke explained to you – the explanation enables you to get the joke, but at the expense of proper appreciation; you get the joke but you aren't amused.

There might well be a further fact about Ann that gets in the way of her appreciation. Perhaps she's just not *intellectual* in the sense we introduced above: perhaps she's just not interested in philosophical ideas. Ann, let's now assume, has a perfectly adequate grasp of Descartes' cogito argument, having done a year's philosophy at university, but still it doesn't really interest her; philosophy has always been much too abstract and abstruse for her taste. (Why on earth should one need to *prove* that one exists, one might ask!) In which case, we suggest, Ann would 'get' the idea, but it wouldn't really engage her interest, very much as one might get the joke without it begin explained, but still one isn't amused by it.

Now let's consider two other famous works of conceptual art which are philosophically knowing, and which also require of Ann the same kind of knowledge and interest as the Trockel piece. First, there is Joseph Kosuth's *One and Three Chairs* (Figure 1.4), which we are already familiar with. This work requires a reasonable knowledge of certain deep metaphysical questions concerning the nature of reality – questions raised by Plato in many of his dialogues, including Book X of *Republic*. Plato argued that, contrary to appearances, the ordinary material things that we find in the world are really a second order, or lower level, of reality. The first level of reality, the highest level, is what Plato called that of 'the forms', the eternal types of which material things are just instances or tokens. So when Socrates asks what a chair is, for example, it's no good just pointing to an instance of a chair, what he's after is the form of the chair, its *essence*, perhaps approximating to what you might find in a definition, of which all material chairs are just instances. Then there is a third level of reality below that to which ordinary material things such as chairs belong: a picture or drawing or shadow of a chair. This is for Plato the third level of reality.[75]

At first, then, you might think that Kosuth's *One and Three Chairs* contains all three levels of reality: the definition (or essence) of a chair, a chair as material object, and the photocopy of a chair. But there's more to Kosuth's piece than this. For Plato also thought that all art was mere representation; art as *mimesis* could never, so to speak, raise itself above the third level of reality. So Kosuth, in taking the definition of the chair (the first level of reality) and the material chair (the second level) and including them in an artwork, thereby turned them into the third level of reality, no more real than the photocopy. The artwork, *One and Three Chairs*, like all artworks, is at three removes from reality.[76]

Ann would need to have knowledge of all this philosophical background if she is properly to appreciate this work of Kosuth's. And, just as with Trockel's piece, she would also need to have a philosophical interest. So she might here too 'get' the idea but not be engaged in it.

Our third example of a philosophically knowing work of conceptual art is *An Oak Tree*, by Michael Craig-Martin. This work (Figure 4.1) consists of a glass of water on a perfectly ordinary bathroom shelf, situated about 3 metres high on the wall. But this is not all. There is a sign nearby which says that the work was called *An Oak Tree*, and (citing from Tony Godfrey's *Conceptual Art*, page 248), 'There was only one other thing in the gallery: a sheet of paper with a series of anonymous questions and answers on it':

Q: To begin with could you describe this work?
A: Yes, of course. What I've done is change a glass of water into a full-grown oak tree without altering the accidents of the glass of water.
Q: The accidents?
A: Yes. The colour, feel, weight, size.
Q: Haven't you simply called this glass of water an oak tree?

A: Absolutely not. It is not a glass of water anymore. I have changed its actual substance. It would no longer be accurate to call it a glass of water. One could call it anything one wished but that would not alter the fact that it is an oak tree. . .

Q: Do you consider that changing the glass of water into an oak tree constitutes an artwork?

A: Yes.

This work is concerned with *transubstantiation*. This is a fact that is revealed to us by the supporting discourse. (So the work is discourse-dependent, in the sense that understanding of it depends on the words written on the sheet of paper on the wall.)

Transubstantiation is a philosophically and theologically difficult notion, as any Catholic will know. Roughly, it's the idea that the bread and wine of the Eucharist changes into the body and blood of Christ. It's not merely a symbolic act. The bread and wine remain the same in their external appearance – in what is called their 'accidents' – but they become different substances: thus the term, 'transubstantiation' (in Latin 'transsubstantiatio'). So those who believe in transubstantiation believe that Christ's saying of the bread and wine, 'This is my body, this is my blood', is to be understood literally.

The accompanying text to *An Oak Tree* shows just how philosophically knowing this piece is: the technical use of the term 'accident' and 'substance'; and the denial that what is being done is merely effecting a change in verbal description ('one could call it anything one wished'). And then there is the fascinating claim that, it seems, it's the artist who has achieved this transubstantiation. The artist, it seems, can turn anything into anything (or is its being a glass of water a necessary starting-place to become an oak tree?).

Now, the appropriate appreciation of *An Oak Tree* requires quite a lot of Ann. She must understand these rudiments of transubstantiation, and she must be intellectually engaged with them. Just as with *One and Three Chairs* and *Cogito Ergo Sum*, it's a work that doesn't seem to be open to everyone for appreciation, or at least not without some prior information. Having said that, this in itself doesn't detract from the merit of these works; to our minds, all three works are fascinating. But if we're right in our discussion, they are *intellectual* works that mightn't be for everyone, very much as philosophy is an intellectual subject that isn't for everyone.

Even if someone is deeply immersed in philosophy and in the difficult notion of transubstantiation, it might still be a matter of individual differences in character and personality whether one gets much from *An Oak Tree*. Not every such philosopher will be able to think better about transubstantiation, or will always find his or her intellectual dispositions enhanced, by contemplating *An Oak Tree*. The philosopher who has already thought deep and long about transubstantiation shouldn't forget what a struggle it was to get to where she now is intellectually. She should look with understanding on her excellent graduate student who has a reproduction of *An Oak Tree* pinned to the wall above his desk to help him to think about the difficult philosophical notions which are involved, and to help him to get his intellectual dispositions to a level approaching those of his mentor whom he so much admires. Moreover, she should think of all those people who don't aspire to be philosophers, and who find philosophical discourse and argument utterly unintelligible, but who are nevertheless profoundly intrigued intellectually by philosophical ideas; these people too might be helped to gain a grasp of the idea of transubstantiation through contemplating *An Oak Tree*.

This is an important conclusion, we think, and in many ways these works do mark a significant break with traditional art. Of course many works of traditional art require background knowledge – for example, of the bible or of myths (consider for example Pieter Breugel's *Landscape with the Fall of Icarus*), and some are quite clearly philosophical. But these traditional works, even if they require the same kind of philosophical knowledge and intellectual interest that is required of Ann in her engagement with the conceptual art pieces, they also use the medium of traditional art to communicate their artistic statement.[77] Conceptual art, in contrast, has nothing to offer except philosophical ideas. And whilst philosophical knowledge is something that one can gain through effort, having intellectual interest seems to be a kind of psychological disposition that one either has or doesn't have, so that extra effort from Ann may well not change her attitude.

The question we now have to ask ourselves is whether Ann really is missing out on something due to her lack of interest in these philosophically knowing works of conceptual art? There are two answers here. One is that she is indeed missing something, for they are philosophically interesting works – as we hope we have shown. What is more, given the right kind of knowledge and interest, the appreciation of these works may well give rise to aesthetic pleasure of the kind we have been discussing: not aesthetic pleasure in the traditional sense, but pleasure in the philosophical ideas which are presented to us. Furthermore, there is also room for intellectual emotions such as the non-aesthetic interest that can be involved in engagement with intellectual ideas.[78]

On the other hand, given the fact that Ann's dispositions of character and personality are as they are (her interests being in the sciences and not in philosophy), there is a sense in which *she* isn't really missing something. The point – and the italicization of the 'she' – is a subtle one, and is worth dwelling on for a moment. Let's contrast appreciation of these works of conceptual art with the appreciation of *The Absinthe Drinker*. This latter work, we suggest, ought to be accessible to *anyone* to appreciate. Imagine that someone said of *The Absinthe Drinker* that they weren't interested in such things as the suffering and loneliness of the human condition, or that they could see the idea that the work is trying to express but they aren't particular moved by it emotionally. We think the right thing to say here is that this person really is missing something, *whatever her dispositions of character and personality*. In contrast, we are suggesting, a work such as *One and Three Chairs* isn't accessible for *anyone* to appreciate; and Ann, being the way *she* is, isn't missing anything.

If this is right, then the important conclusion is that some (not necessarily all) works of conceptual art that are philosophically knowing simply aren't for everyone, and that this marks a contrast with some (not necessarily all) works of traditional art. However, it's important to remember that we haven't tried to generalise this argument, to draw a contrast between *all* conceptual art and *all* traditional art.

CONCEPTUAL ART AND EMOTIONAL ENGAGEMENT

Not all works of conceptual art are intellectual, or philosophically knowing. Some seek to engage our emotions in ways quite similar to certain traditional works – that is, to engage our non-intellectual emotions. Let's consider an example.[79]

In September 2002 invitations were sent out to members of the art scene to attend the opening of the £500,000 extension of the Lisson Gallery in London. When the guests turned up, ready for their usual fare of champagne and canapés, what they found instead was that the whole of the front of the gallery was boarded up by a large expanse of corrugated iron, with no means of entrance. The guests were at first puzzled, and then many of them became angry and frustrated at being shut out. Finally, the artist, Santiago Sierra, emerged and told them that this *was* the exhibit, called *Space Closed by Corrugated Metal* (Figure 5.2). Sierra was quoted in *The Guardian* as saying: 'It was part of a broader work which is a commentary on frustration at not being able to get in somewhere for economic or political reasons.' *The Guardian* continues: 'It was prompted by events in Argentina, where, following the collapse of the peso, banks

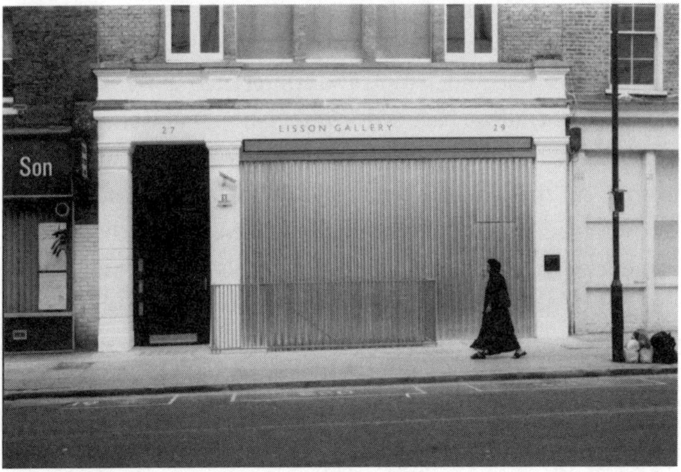

Figure 5.2 Santiago Sierra, *Space Closed by Corrugated Metal*.

Santiago Sierra, Space Closed by Corrugated Metal, Lisson Gallery, London. September 2002. Courtesy the artist and Lisson Gallery pulled corrugated sheets across their buildings to stop people from withdrawing their savings'.[80]

There are several things to note about this work. First, it is discourse-dependent. Second, the event at which the work was introduced to the public was designed in order to engage the non-intellectual emotions of anger and frustration in the audience, and thereby to get them to appreciate better what it might be like to find oneself unable to withdraw one's savings. Even if we weren't part of the audience who first experienced the work, and thus didn't have those feelings of anger and frustration, we can still appreciate the work (the piece) aided by means such as 'documentation', photographs and other supporting information (such as is provided here in this book). For we can imagine what it would have been like to be one of those who was actually present, and this would enable us better to imagine what it would be like to be unable to withdraw our savings.

Acconci's *Following Piece* (Figure 1.2), which we have already discussed, can be understood and appreciated in the same kind of way. Again, all we have is documentation, but through using our imagination we can gain an idea of what it would be like to find out that we had been followed as we walk innocently through the streets.[81] Perhaps the work can then be read as something of a commentary on the multiple intrusions into our privacy these days (much more now than in the 1960s when the work was made) – hidden cameras, and so on – to which we can respond with emotions such as fear and resentment.

So these two works of conceptual art aren't purely intellectual, nor are they philosophically knowing, and they do seek to engage our non-intellectual emotions and imagination in ways that philosophically knowing works of conceptual art do not. The important message this reveals is just how wrong it would be to condemn all conceptual art as not 'for me' just because, rather like Ann, you aren't interested in philosophy or in philosophical ideas. These works of Sierra's and Acconci's ought to be able to reach out to all of us in the same way as Degas' *The Absinthe Drinker*.

One should admit, however, that the interest and pleasures that we can get from these works of conceptual art – even works such as *Space Closed* – aren't perhaps as easily won as the interest and pleasures that we get from much traditional art. Often, we have to work harder – a short passing glance is by no means enough – and the rejection of all physical media makes the route to these pleasures entirely non-perceptual. But two points are worth making here. First, many works of traditional art are by no means easily accessible (many of the works of Claude Poussin for example), and conversely many works of conceptual art are really quite readily understood (Warhol's *Brillo Boxes* perhaps). Secondly, we shouldn't forget that the short passing glance at familiar traditional art is too short: familiarity here breeds not contempt but complacency. A work such as *The Absinthe Drinker* might *seem* easily accessible, but surely we cannot attain the potential depth and range of emotional engagement merely with a passing glance. So perhaps we can learn something about more familiar traditional art from thinking about (the often less familiar) conceptual art: appreciation of good art takes time.

THE COGNITIVE VALUE OF CONCEPTUAL ART

We saw in earlier chapters that the domain of the artistic extends beyond the domain of the aesthetic. Correspondingly, the domain of artistic *value* extends beyond the domain of aesthetic value, where aesthetic value is understood in the traditional sense. So in the light of this, let's consider again the philosophically knowing works of conceptual art that we've been looking at, and ask what kind of artistic value they might have.

Most philosophers would agree that one important kind of artistic value is *cognitive value*. Cognitive value is the value that an artwork possesses in virtue of its being able in some way to convey or yield knowledge to those who engage with it. The idea, then, is that one of the main reasons why many of us do value art is because of the way in which it can help us to understand certain things about the world and its inhabitants. This knowledge can, as we will soon see, take many forms, ranging from factual knowledge about certain historical events, say, to a deeper insight into how people who have had different kinds of experiences see the world. Art, then, is valuable to us at least partly because it adds something to the way in which we understand things, people and events around us.

However, and in spite of what we've been saying so far, it is by no means straightforward to explain how conceptual art can have cognitive value *as art*. And there are arguments that we'll need to consider which purport to show that it cannot.

Let's begin, not with conceptual art, but with traditional art, and with paintings and fictional literature in particular. How can these provide knowledge? One idea here is that they can provide knowledge by *showing* us things about the world.[82] Considering again *The Absinthe Drinker* (Figure 5.1), this picture shows us the loneliness of life, and it does so in a way that we might otherwise not have fully appreciated in all its depths.[83] In this way, we can gain knowledge from the work. Similarly, we can gain knowledge from fiction (putting to one side here the kinds of factual knowledge one can gain from fiction, as one can gain factual knowledge of the whaling industry from *Moby Dick*, or knowledge of the condition of the working class in Victorian Manchester from *Mary Barton*). For example, Joseph Conrad's *Lord Jim* shows us how one can be tortured by feelings of shame and guilt for a past wrongdoing, and how these feelings can endure over a lifetime, and ultimately lead to one's ruin.

So to allow that works such as these can convey knowledge, we need to understand the process of gaining knowledge as consisting of more than just coming to believe truths in the right way. With *The Absinthe Drinker* we don't simply come to know *that* life is lonely; for after all life can be joyfully full of real companionship (as some other pictures ably portray). Rather, we come to gain a grasp of what loneliness is like, even (or especially) whilst in the company of others. This knowledge – what is sometimes appropriately called what-it-is-like knowledge – is a kind of knowledge that is not fully captured by the notion of coming to believe truths in the right way.[84]

Hopefully, this discussion of how we can gain knowledge from traditional artworks will have reminded you of Sierra's *Space Closed* and Acconci's *Following Piece*. These works of conceptual art help you to gain what-it-is-like knowledge: of what it is like to be angry and frustrated by being unable to gain access to what one has a right to gain access to; and of what it is like to find out that one was being followed in a public place without having done anything wrong. Appreciation of these works requires imagination, no doubt, and this use of our imagination is part of what it is to engage in the right way with the cognitive value of art – whether conceptual or traditional. And engaging with the cognitive value of art in the right way is bound up with many other kinds of intellectual engagement: imaginative and emotional (including engaging the intellectual emotions) as well as aesthetic.

A difficulty arises here, which can apply to both traditional and conceptual art. Let's take *Space Closed*. Many of us – perhaps most of us – already know what it is like to experience anger and frustration at being locked out and excluded from a place where we consider we have a right to be. So in what sense can we be said to *gain* knowledge here? The answer is that we need a broader notion of the cognitive value of art that goes beyond the mere gaining of knowledge, whether it is factual knowledge or what-it-is-like knowledge. Art can also have cognitive value by *improving* and *deepening* our knowledge and, more broadly still, our intellectual skills and virtues.[85] *Space Closed* puts us in a special position to *reflect* on the experience of what it must be like to be unable to get in somewhere for economic or political reasons; and we can reflect on how many people around the world find themselves in such a dire position. The emotional experience that the work engenders is sufficiently complex and rich for us to be able to return to the work in imagination on several occasions in order further to enrich our knowledge and understanding through this kind of reflection.

A further point is relevant here. Engagement with the cognitive value of art should be seen as bound up with the many other ways in which we engage with art. As Matthew Kieran puts it:

> Assessing works in terms of their insight, profundity, complexity, interest, coherence, consistency, depth or intelligibility, or their sentimentality, callowness, banality or naivety, involves a cluster of notions that are mutually interdependent, amongst which is the notion of truth. Works

can indeed be profound yet mistaken, or true to life yet banal; insights can be partial.[86]

COGNITIVE VALUE AND DISCOURSE-DEPENDENCE

So far, then, we have not seen any significant difference between cognitive value in traditional art and cognitive value in conceptual art: conceptual art, like traditional art, can have cognitive value by *showing* us things about the world. But further difficulties and concerns have to be dealt with when we turn to discourse-dependent works, which seem to be particularly prevalent in conceptual art. Discourse-dependent works are those works of art that depend on discourse, either as part of the work itself, or a surrounding or background discourse or narrative, in order to be properly appreciated. Duchamp's *Fountain* is discourse-dependent, as it cannot be appreciated through inspection of the urinal on its own: we need also to know the history of the work's making – what we have called the work-narrative. Trockel's *Cogito Ergo Sum* is discourse-dependent, as is *Space Closed*, *Following Piece* and *An Oak Tree*: appreciation of each of them depends in one way or another on background knowledge that cannot be gained through inspection of the physical object or the physical record of the performance alone.

This first concern about discourse-dependent conceptual art is especially prominent in works of conceptual art that are autobiographical. This is the case with, for example, many of the works of Tracey Emin, which depend on knowledge of aspects of the artist's life for their proper appreciation.[87] One can feel excluded, as if one is listening in to a private confession. But this is perhaps just an extreme case of what is a frequent complaint about conceptual art – that it is esoteric, or intended for appreciation by the initiated only: the art world talking to the art world, as it is often remarked. At its extreme, there does seem to be something objectionable about this kind of work; this esoteric kind of discourse dependence does seem to get in the way of appreciation – assuming that is, that there is something worthwhile to be appreciated at all.

Generally speaking, though, and abstracting from these extreme examples, there is no good reason why the fact that a work is discourse-dependent should be a hindrance to its having cognitive value. It might well be a hindrance if one is operating with an unduly narrow notion of knowledge as consisting only of true belief acquired in a certain way. For it is generally accepted that part of what it is to acquire knowledge of truths in the right way is in some sense to arrive at those beliefs in a way that is justified, through *argument* of the right kind, and the discourse surrounding conceptual art doesn't provide argument.[88] But, as we've seen earlier, an artwork's having cognitive value isn't restricted to its yielding knowledge in the form of true beliefs that have been arrived at in the right way. Artworks can also be cognitively valuable in that they *facilitate* knowledge, and enhance and deepen our intellectual skills and virtues. This broader conception of cognitive value, possessed by many good conceptual artworks, also helps to explain an important phenomenon which we remarked on earlier: as with much traditional art, we can return to these artworks time after time and *continue* to find cognitive value in them, and this could not be explained if all they yielded were knowledge of facts.

A second concern with discourse-dependent conceptual artworks is this: if cognitive value depends so much on the discourse, isn't the artwork itself redundant? And if so, why should we attribute any value to the artwork as such, particularly bearing in mind that it lacks aesthetic value in the traditional sense? The answer to this returns us to the idea idea. The artwork, in conceptual art, involves the ideas which comprise the medium by which the artist makes his artistic statement. So we have in no way made the artwork itself redundant; to think so is to confuse the artwork itself with something else – with the physical thing perhaps, or with the performance, which is just the means by which the artist communicates his or her idea. Without the artwork – that is to say, without the ideas and the artistic statement – the background discourse would be of no artistic value.

The third concern with discourse-dependent conceptual artworks will get us closer to our final thoughts about conceptual art. In a way it takes us back to questions of definition that we discussed in Chapter two. Our idea has been that works such as *One and Three Chairs* and *An Oak Tree* raise deeply interesting philosophical questions, and that they have cognitive value in virtue of the way in which they raise these questions. Here's the concern. Someone might equally well rig up something like *One and Three Chairs* as part of a philosophy lecture on Plato's *Republic*. So why should we say that it is as a piece of *art* that what we are presented with has cognitive value?

The concern can be articulated in a slightly different way. When a traditional artwork which has cognitive value also has aesthetic value in the traditional sense, then it is generally accepted – and surely rightly so – that it has cognitive value *as art*. But when we turn to the cognitive value of conceptual artworks, the question of why it is *as art* that it has cognitive value becomes especially pressing. At this point it won't help to appeal to Aesthetic Idealism and the aesthetic value of ideas, for it has been accepted that ideas can have aesthetic value outside art too: recall the elegance of the mathematical proof.

So what is it that makes the cognitive value of *One and Three Chairs*' cognitive part of its *artistic* value? The fact that conceptual art might in some way satisfy the requirements of an institutional definition seems to be something of a verbal point here. In a sense this move gets the concern back to front. For we are left with the deeper and more pressing question of what art, as art, is *meant* to do? And does conceptual art do what art is meant to do?

IS ART MEANT TO FULFIL SOME HUMAN NEED?

One of the things we have been arguing in this book is that we shouldn't rush to make blanket judgements about conceptual art. Sometimes we might be tempted to do so, as a kind of visceral response to the feelings of fear and doubt that conceptual art can give rise to, but it is important that we resist the temptation. It is no more appropriate to make blanket generalisations about conceptual art than it is to make blanket generalisations about traditional art.

The danger with generalisations arises when they are taken (mistaken) to be universal claims, and in this book we have been critical of arguments against conceptual art that aspire to universality. But still, we should not be afraid to make generalisations just so long as it is accepted, by both speaker and audience, that they are only to be applied 'for the most part'. Indeed, generalisations are an important way of thinking about the world. (It was a *criticism* of Florence Nightingale when Lytton Strachey said of her that 'she was never at home with a generalisation'.[89]) So it's with this caveat in mind that we want to explore our final idea: good conceptual art (for the most part) fails to satisfy certain deep human needs which good traditional art (for the most part) does satisfy. Putting the point another way, conceptual art might well be good *as conceptual art* but still it might not be good art, perhaps precisely because it fails to satisfy these needs.

What might these deep human needs be? There are (at least) four possible approaches to this question. First, we might say that there is a deep human need for pleasure, and we can get pleasure from the beauty of good art – in other words, aesthetic pleasure in the traditional sense. But there are difficulties with this approach. To begin with, we have already seen that there is much of value in art beyond beauty. We value the German expressionists for their brutal, open-eyed portrayal of the ugliness of the world during and after the First World War, and these works don't give rise to *pleasure*. What is more, we can value art, including much traditional art, because of its intellectual interest and because of the intellectual emotions that it engenders – emotions that are other than pleasure. And finally, it isn't so far clear why art as a source of pleasure couldn't be replaced by other sources of pleasure, such as sport or games. We need to look deeper.

A second possible approach is to appeal to evolution and the idea that art helps us to survive as a species. Art seems to be a universal feature, appearing in all cultures, from the earliest traces of human activity. So perhaps art is an *adaptation*, as some anthropologists have argued. For something to be an adaptation, it must contribute to our fitness and to our reproductive success.[90] One idea here is that the artist's skill is like the famous peacock's tail: a peacock with a fine plumage is more likely to attract a mate, and is more likely to pass on its genes because its chances of reproducing are thus enhanced. Another idea is that the presence of art helps to sustain an environment in which its members flourish, and thereby enhances reproductive success. This environment is of the kind, as the philosopher Stephen Davies puts it, 'in which there is mutual support and respect, a shared sense of belonging and caring, stability, self-confirmation, a feeling of control or accommodation with nature, and so on'.[91] The difficulty with this possible approach is not that evolutionary accounts of art are false. Indeed, there is very likely to be a true evolutionary explanation of art, given its universality. The difficulty, rather, is that this account does not address *our* deep human needs – needs that are part of *our* psychology – and this is where our interests lie here.

A third possible approach avoids the difficulties of the first two. This approach would look to a Freudian account of our deep drives, showing how art satisfies these deep drives.[92] We will remain neutral about this approach, for a Freudian account, like an evolutionary account, can be, and ought to be, consistent with an account of our actual human psychology that is accessible to us in a way that our Freudian drives are not.

So let's now turn to the explanation that we do favour – one to which, we hope, we all can resonate as an accessible part of our own psychology. The idea is that art – needless to say *good* art – helps us to appreciate our own humanity in a special way. This is what art is meant to do. The philosopher Anthony Savile, in a very nice article, draws on Immanuel Kant's marvellous phrase, that our imagination, here deployed in artistic activity, 'enables us to construct a second nature out of the material made by actual nature'.[93] Of course, imagination can be deployed in other ways too, but there is something special about art. What is special about art, Savile says, is that:

> second nature is presented as if it were actual nature. Thus the spectator is presented with a view of some topic or theme as already imbued with significance, one which in the

case of beautiful art moves him to adjust his ways of thinking about and responding in feeling to that theme as it (potentially) occurs in real life itself.[94]

Art, then, presents to us human life and the world in which we live in this special way – as 'second nature'. And things are different afterwards, when we return to actual nature, to the world beyond art. As Savile writes, '[t]he work of art can have a deep sense for us only if it exercises its force when we are no longer in its presence, if it modifies our dispositions to think, to feel, and ultimately to act' (page 253).

This does not just involve art presenting first nature to us as beautiful.[95] As Richard Wollheim has said, an exclusive focus on beauty 'would exclude much of the material that has inspired the artist of the last hundred and fifty years: the modern city, and its teeming chaos, the life of the poor and the outcast, sexuality in all its varieties, violence, suffering and war, and the mute tribute exacted by quiet domesticity'.[96] Remember Picasso's *Guernica*, Degas' *The Absinthe Drinker*, and the German expressionists.

So art – *good* art – presents to us, as 'second nature', human nature in all its varieties. But why should its doing this fulfil some deep human need? Here is at least a partial answer.

Human life, and the world in which we live, are presented to us through art in a way which we can see as shared with others. It makes us see that not only the beautiful things in life, but also the terrible (the violence, suffering, war and so on), are things to which we respond in ways that we can and do share with others. First, we can see that they are shared with the artist who presented them to us as 'second nature'. And secondly, we can see them as shareable with others who are, or could be, engaged with the art – not just with those of our own time and culture but also (and often) more widely, across times and across cultures.

So art can give us a sense of our shared humanity in a special way, relating what is presented to us to our ethical lives, in the broadest possible sense of the word 'ethical'. And in doing this it relates us to each other. As Joseph Conrad put it, the artist speaks to

> the subtle but invincible conviction of solidarity that knits together the loneliness of innumerable hearts; to the solidarity in dreams, in joy, in sorrow, in aspiration, in illusions, in hope, in fear, which binds men to each other, which binds together all humanity – the dead to the living and the living to the unborn.[97]

A very special instance of shared responses, according to Kant, is in our aesthetic judgements. These command universal agreement in a particularly strong way, he says. It is this, in part, that marks off aesthetic judgements from mere expressions of preference. Of course, it doesn't follow that everyone *will* agree, but an aesthetic judgement is such that 'a person who describes something as beautiful insists that every one *ought* to give the object in question his approval and follow suit in describing it as beautiful'.[98]

Kant thought that, in making properly universalisable aesthetic judgements in this way, we ought to 'abstract from charm and emotion'.[99] Perhaps this is right, perhaps there is a special way in which aesthetic judgements abstracted from charm and emotion ought to be shared by all humanity. But Conrad is thinking of our broader responses to art when he speaks of 'the subtle but invincible conviction of solidarity'. For example, let's assume with Kant that the feelings of desolation and loneliness that we have in response to *The Absinthe*

Drinker aren't part of the aesthetic judgement itself. And let's assume, also with Kant, that these feelings don't command universal assent in precisely the same way as an aesthetic judgement. Yet we can still agree with Conrad's wonderful sentiments. If when you look at *The Absinthe Drinker* your heart is not knitted together with the loneliness of innumerable other hearts, then you are, indeed, missing something.

Where, then, does conceptual art (remember that we are *generalising* here) fall short? Perhaps conceptual art falls short because it restricts itself to engaging our intellectual interests and emotions. (So Sierra's *Space Closed* wouldn't fall under this generalisation.) And our intellectual interests and emotions in response to conceptual art are limited in their scope. First, they cannot be expected to reach out to 'all humanity', to each one of us; remember that conceptual art is not for everyone – not for Ann, for example. Secondly, even if a particular piece of conceptual art engenders intellectual interests and emotions that happen to be shared by each one of us, it won't have the resources to address the shared aesthetic responses and pleasures which traditional art affords. Nor will it have the resources to extend beyond the aesthetic to include the whole gamut of shared human thought, feeling, and emotionality – our dreams, our joys, our sorrows, our aspirations, our illusions, our hopes, our fears.

WHERE WE'VE BEEN

In our journey we hope we have shown that conceptual art, and the idea idea, really does represent a significant break with traditional art – a more significant one than we find from other kinds of art that have gone before. This isn't surprising because many of the conceptual artists whose work we've been looking at have explicitly set out to challenge art's received wisdom and traditional, orthodox notions. Connected with this is the fact that so much conceptual art is philosophically knowing, for conceptual artists often turned to philosophy to help them to make good their challenges. These two features of conceptual art – challenging received traditions, and being philosophically knowing – explain in part why there has been quite a lot of philosophy in this book. Also, we hope to have shown, thinking about conceptual art from a philosophically informed perspective helps one to think about philosophy of art more widely, and to see more clearly what are the kinds of presuppositions that ground our commonsense attitudes towards our appreciation of traditional art – attitudes that might otherwise have gone unexamined. Philosophical understanding of art can work in the service of the appreciation of art.

Although we have good reason to approach the appreciation of conceptual art in a different way to the way in which we approach the appreciation of traditional art, this doesn't imply that one has good reason to be generally dismissive of conceptual art – even if not all conceptual art is for everyone. One should appreciate, or even *celebrate*, its differences from past traditions, rather than insisting that all conceptual art is inferior just because it's not like what has gone before. For there is no doubt that conceptual art does offer a lot that is of value, including intellectual appreciation of ideas (philosophical ideas in particular).

But still, there is one especially significant difference which we think is often central to an explanation of why so many of us, and so often, fail to be fully satisfied by conceptual art: its rejection of the traditional notion of the aesthetic. Conceptual art does not provide – does not set out to provide – the kind of aesthetic pleasures and emotions that are so familiar to all of us from good traditional art, and which we can so readily share with each other, across times and across cultures, as part of our common humanity. Conceptual art's not being aesthetic in this traditional sense might well represent a failure to fulfil a deep human need that we find satisfied elsewhere in art. Whilst this is no reason to dismiss conceptual art out of hand as having *no* artistic value, nor is it a reason to be afraid of it, its lacking aesthetic value in this traditional sense might nonetheless be a reason why conceptual art – even good conceptual art – is not wholly successful *as art*.

Notes

1 J. L. Austin, 'A Plea for Excuses', in his *Philosophical Papers*, 3rd edn. Oxford: Oxford University Press, 1970, 175–205, at 185.

2 Mel Ramsden in 'Memories of the Medicine Show', *Art-Language* New Series 2, 1997, 32.

3 There are some excellent books which chart the history of conceptual art better than we could hope to do here. See, for example, Lucy Lippard, *Six Years: The Dematerialization of the Art Object from 1966 to 1972*, California: University of California Press, 1973 and Daniel Marzona, *Conceptual Art: Brilliant Concepts*, Taschen Basic Arts Series.

4 There are various places where this story can be found. See, for example, Tony Godfrey's *Conceptual Art*. London: Phaidon Press, 1998.

5 Thanks to Tony Godfrey's *Conceptual Art* for this citation. A full account of all Duchamp's preparatory work in setting up the rejection of *Fountain* is in Chapter 2 of Thierry De Duve's *Kant After Duchamp*. Cambridge, MA: MIT Press, 1996.

6 See, for example, the discussion of Clement Greenberg in Arthur Danto's *After the End of Art: Contemporary Art and the Pale of History*. Princeton: Princeton University Press, 1997, Chapter 4.

7 We are grateful to an anonymous referee for this example.

8 Cited by Joseph Kosuth in his 'Art after Philosophy', *Studio International*, 1969.

9 In Clement Greenberg, *The Collected Essays and Criticisms Volume 4: Modernism with a Vengeance 1957–69*. Edited by J. O'Brian. Chicago: University of Chicago Press, 1993, 86–87.

10 Tom Wolfe, *The Painted Word*. New York: Bantam Books, 1975, 41.

11 In fact there are perceptible differences if you get up close – thus the parenthetic 'virtually'.

12 Arthur Danto, *The Transfiguration of the Commonplace*. Cambridge, MA: Harvard University Press, 1981.

13 See her *Six Years: The Dematerialization of the Art Object*.

14 In Ancient Greek, the term 'aesthesis' referred to sensuous perception. It wasn't until Alexander Baumgarten published his *Aesthetica* in 1750 that the word began to refer to beauty and the notion of the aesthetic as we think of it today, significantly influenced of course by Kant's *Critique of Judgement*, first published 1790. Translated by James Creed Meredith. Oxford: Clarendon Press, 1952.

15 Marcel Duchamp, 'Apropos of "Readymades"', cited in Tony Godfrey's *Conceptual Art*, 27–28.

16 Joseph Kosuth, 'Art after Philosophy', *Studio International*, 1969.

17 Harking back to our earlier discussion of consciousness, it might he interesting to think through just why your computer's coming up with 'cogito ergo sum' when it is turned on is not proof of its existence, whereas your coming up with those words when you wake up in the morning is such a proof. (What if you had been hypnotised to say the words every morning?)

18 Perhaps this also is true of Trockel's piece: the black square is clearly intended to remind the knowing viewer of the black squares of Ad Reinhardt, such as his *Abstract Painting No. 5* (1962).

19 Kosuth, 'Art after philosophy', *Studio International* 178, 1969, cited in Carolyn Wilde's 'Matter and meaning in the work of art: Joseph Kosuth's *One and Three Chairs*', in *Philosophy and Conceptual Art*. Edited by Peter Goldie and Elisabeth Schellekens. Oxford: Oxford University Press, 2007, 119–137.

20 *Transfiguration of the Commonplace*, 56.

21 *The Painted Word*, 92.

22 Sol LeWitt, 'Paragraphs on Conceptual Art', *Artforum* 5 (1967): 79–83.

23 It's important to bear in mind that not all non-conceptual art is traditional – that would be to treat pop art, for example, as traditional. But we will nevertheless often contrast conceptual art with traditional art, whilst not treating the two categories as contraries.

24 Jerry Levinson, 'Refining Art Historically', *Journal of Aesthetics and Art Criticism* 47 (1989): 21–33.

25 As an exercise, try to think of what the necessary and sufficient conditions are for something to be conscious. If you get the right answer, then you will have solved the problem of consciousness!

26 Morris Weitz, 'The Role of Theory in Aesthetics', *Journal of Aesthetics and Art Criticism* 15 (1956): 27–35.

27 William Kennick, 'Does Traditional Aesthetics Rest on a Mistake?', *Mind* 67 (1958): 317–334.

28 For a full discussion and references to other commentaries, see Stephen Davies's very helpful book, *Definitions of Art*. Ithaca: Cornell University Press, 1991.

29 In his *Transfiguration of the Commonplace*, 59. There's a more sympathetic reading of Weitz and Wittgenstein here: that what cannot be defined in terms of necessary and sufficient conditions is family *resemblance*, and not family *membership*. (Thanks to an anonymous referee for pointing this out.) However, this still leaves untouched our main objection, that art cannot be sorted out from non-art by reference only to perceptual resemblance.

30 Originally set out in George Dickie, *The Art Circle: A Theory of Art*. New York: Haven, 1984. The view is recapitulated in his 'The Institutional Theory of Art'. In *Theories of Art Today*. Edited by Noel Carroll. Wisconsin: The University of Wisconsin Press, 2000, 96. For a different approach to defining art institutionally, see a series of articles by Jerrold Levinson: 'Defining Art Historically', *British Journal of Aesthetics* 19 (1979): 232–250; 'Refining Art Historically', *Journal of Aesthetics and Art Criticism* 47 (1989): 21–33, and 'Extending Art Historically', *Journal of Aesthetics and Art Criticism* 51 (1993): 411–423.

31 As Stephen Davies says in his *Definitions of Art*, to which we are much indebted here and elsewhere, 'the classification of things as artworks would seem to reflect a need or concern that we have. Moreover, many if not all artworks are manufactured with that interest in mind', 37.

32 As Davies points out in *Definitions of Art*.

33 See, for example, Berys Gaut '"Art" as a Cluster Concept'. In *Theories of Art Today*. Edited by Noel Carroll. Wisconsin: The University of Wisconsin Press, 2000, 25-44; and Robert Stecker's *Artworks: Definition, Meaning, Value*, University Park, PA: Pennsylvania State University Press, 1997. It's important to distinguish these views from those of Weitz and Kennick, which we considered earlier.

34 This idea is discussed (and rejected) by Dominic McIver Lopes as what he calls the 'New Art Hypothesis', in his 'Conceptual Art is Not What it Seems'. In *Philosophy and Conceptual Art*. Edited by Peter Goldie and Elisabeth Schellekens, 238–256.

35 It's worth remembering that according to George Dickie's institutional definition which we examined earlier, a work of art is an 'artefact'. Does this notion of an artefact include man-made 'things' such thoughts and ideas? We leave that question open.

36 Diderot suggested Falconnet to Catherine the Great as the right person to produce a monument to Peter. The story of Falconnet's efforts, and

of his subsequent falling out with Catherine, is amusingly described in Malcolm Bradbury's *To The Hermitage*, London: Penguin, 2002.

37 London: printed for A. C. and sold by A. Bettesworth, 1725. The punctuation has been modernised from the original.

38 Joseph Kosuth, 1996. 'Intention(s)'. *Art Bulletin* LXXVIII, 1996, p. 412. Also in *Conceptual Art: A Critical Anthology*, Alexander Alberro & Blake Stimson, eds, Cambridge, MA.: MIT Press, 1999, p. 461.

39 'Art After Philosophy', *Studio International* 178 (1969).

40 'Paragraphs on Conceptual Art', *Artforum*, June (1967).

41 Ibid.

42 *The Painted Word*, 92.

43 Thanks to Dom Lopes for bringing this to our attention.

44 See Elisabeth Schellekens, 'The Aesthetic Value of Ideas', in *Philosophy and Conceptual Art*, 77.

45 Lucy Lippard and John Chandler, 'The dematerialization of art', *Art International* 12 (1968): 31–36. Cited in 'The dematerialization of the object' by Derek Matravers, *Philosophy and Conceptual Art*, 18–31.

46 Derek Matravers has a very nice discussion of this in his 'The dematerialization of the object'.

47 See Peter Kivy's *Philosophies of the Arts: An Essay in Differences*, Cambridge: Cambridge University Press, 1993.

48 There are for sure subtleties in the appreciation of Japanese scrolls (for example, the ways in which the poetry is *expressed* in the calligraphy) that we are missing in order to make our central point. Kendall Walton's 'Categories of Art' contains a seminal discussion of these issues; *Philosophical Review* 79 (1970): 334–367.

49 Richard Wollheim has a very good discussion of this in his 'Criticism as retrieval', in his *Art and Its Objects*, Cambridge: Cambridge University Press, 1980, 185–203. In that essay he argues that the whole narrative of how a work of art came to be in existence is relevant to its appreciation, including, but not limited to, the artist's aims and intentions, the traditions from which it sprang, and other aspects of its making and its history in as wide a context as is appropriate.

50 The risqué joke is that the letters pronounced in French sound like 'She has a hot ass!'.

51 This is closely connected to what Ronald de Sousa has called 'Alcmene's problem', named after the faithful wife of Amphitryon. According to the myth, Zeus desired Alcmene, and wanted to seduce her, so when her husband was away, he took on the husband's form in order to fool her, and thereby to have his way with her. De Sousa asks whether she

should mind when she finds out about the trick that has been played on her. De Sousa concludes that she should. See his excellent book *The Rationality of Emotion*, Cambridge, MA: MIT Press, 1987.

52 In his 'On perceiving conceptual art', Peter Lamarque discussed concrete poetry in this context; this essay is in *Philosophy and Conceptual Art*. Edited by Peter Goldie and Elisabeth Schellekens, 3–17. In relation to Japanese calligraphy, appreciation of the markings on the page, as physical medium, is not all there is to appreciation of the work; that's why they are a *medium*.

53 For discussion of this and related ideas, see Robert Hopkins' 'Speaking through silence: Conceptual art and conversational implicature', in *Philosophy and Conceptual Art*, 51–68.

54 'Aesthetic and non-aesthetic', *Philosophical Review*, 74 (1965): 135–159, reprinted in *Frank Sibley: Approach to Aesthetics – Collected Papers*. Edited by John Benson, Betty Redfearn and Jeremy Roxbee Cox. Oxford: Clarendon Press, 33–51. For more information on some recent discussions on the perceptual requirement, see Malcolm Budd, 'The Acquaintance Principle', *British Journal of Aesthetics* 43 (2003): 386–392, and Paisley Livingston, 'On an Apparent Truism in Aesthetics', *British Journal of Aesthetics* 43 (2003): 260–278.

55 Moreover, literature is not specific to any one sense modality: one can gain access to a novel through touch (by reading it in Braille), or through hearing, so it's not necessary to see the novel, the words on the page. Music and painting are not like that: music must be *heard*, paintings must be *seen*.

56 Timothy Binkley, 'Piece Contra Aesthetics', *Journal of Aesthetics and Art Criticism* 35 (1977): 265–277.

57 In this and the following paragraphs – and indeed in the whole of this book – we are greatly indebted to David Davies's excellent book *Art as Performance*. Oxford: Blackwell, 2003. Davies has a very subtle discussion of Acconci's work, especially in Chapters 8 and 9.

58 The film of these performances can be seen at http://dailymotion.alice.it/video/x7ygqa_vito-acconci-three-adaptation-studi_creation

59 Cited by Tony Godfrey in his *Conceptual Art*, 27–28.

60 The distinction between these two kinds of concept was first made in these terms by Bernard Williams in his *Ethics and the Limits of Philosophy*. London: Fontana Press, 1985, 129–130 and 140–142. Williams' contrast was concerned with ethical properties, but much the same distinction can be made amongst aesthetic properties.

61 Thanks to Jaegwon Kim for this way of putting it. A helpful discussion of dependence bases, supervenience, and related notions is in Kim's

Supervenience and Mind: Selected Philosophical Essays. Cambridge: Cambridge University Press, 1993.

62 Roberta Smith, 'Conceptual Art', in *Concepts of Modern Art*. Edited by Nikos Stangos. London: Thames and Hudson, 1994, 260.

63 In Danto's collected essays *Unnatural Wonders: Essays from the Gap between Art and Life*, New York: Columbia University Press, 2005, 323.

64 We are grateful here to Nick Zangwill's *Aesthetic Creation*, Oxford: Oxford University Press, 2007, in which he argues for a version of what we are calling Aesthetic Traditionalism. We don't want to suggest, however, that the way we set out the arguments for Aesthetic Traditionalism is one that Zangwill would endorse.

65 This requirement on a good definition is sometimes called 'extensional adequacy'; for discussion, see Zangwill's *Aesthetic Creation*, Chapter 3.

66 We take this to be at the heart of Zangwill's view in *Aesthetic Creation*.

67 Of course it needs to be focused in order to have something worthwhile and interesting to say – a point well made by Zangwill in *Aesthetic Creation*, 74. Zangwill is concerned only to respond to the threat from art that doesn't have aesthetic properties. We, in contrast, are also concerned with art that has aesthetic properties and that also has other artistic properties that are an important part of its artistic value; to our mind, such artworks are as much a threat to aesthetic traditionalism as are the former kind.

68 This is discussed in David Thompson's fascinating *Have You Seen. . .?*, London: Allen Lane.

69 In *Aesthetic Creation*, 62.

70 Other urinals from the same warehouse won't have Duchamp's signature on them, but we will ignore this difference here.

71 These issues are discussed in detail in Elisabeth Schellekens' 'The Aesthetic Value of Ideas', in *Philosophy and Conceptual Art*, 71–91, in Dermot Costello's 'Kant after LeWitt: Towards an Aesthetics of Conceptual Art' in the same volume, 92–115, and in James Shelley's 'The Problem of Non-Perceptual Art', *British Journal of Aesthetics* 43 (2003): 363–378.

72 In his *Ethics, Evil, and Fiction*, Oxford: Clarendon Press, 1997, 92–93.

73 For more information on the metaphoric use of aesthetic terms, see Roger Scruton, *Art and Imagination*, London: Routledge & Kegan, 1982, and Nick Zangwill, 'Metaphor and Realism in Aesthetics', *Journal of Aesthetics and Art Criticism* 49 (1991): 57–62.

74 Michael Stocker uses this definition in his 'Intellectual and Other Non-Standard Emotions', in *The Oxford Handbook of Philosophy of Emotion*. Edited by Peter Goldie, Oxford: Oxford University Press, 2009. See also Stocker's 'Some Considerations about Intellectual Desire and Emotions',

in *Thinking about Feeling: Contemporary Philosophers on Emotion*. Edited by Robert C. Solomon, Oxford: Oxford University Press, 2004, 135–150.

75 For more reading on Plato, see Julia Annas, *Plato: A Very Short Introduction*, Oxford: Oxford University Press, 2003, or the entry on Plato in the online *Stanford Encyclopaedia of Philosophy* by Richard Kraut.

76 See Carolyn Wilde's excellent discussion in her 'Matter and meaning in the work of art', in *Philosophy and Conceptual Art*.

77 An example here is certain Byzantine art, which is often directly concerned with complex theological and philosophical issues (such as the nature of the holy trinity), much in the way that Craig-Martin's work is. However, these ideas in Byzantine art are mediated through traditional artistic media. Thanks to an anonymous referee for this helpful example.

78 See Michael Stocker's discussion of intellectual emotions in his 'Some Considerations about Intellectual Desire and Emotion', in *Thinking about Feeling*.

79 See Peter Goldie's discussion in 'Conceptual art and knowledge', in *Philosophy and Conceptual Art*, 157–170.

80 *The Guardian* October 11, 2002.

81 There are interesting questions here about the kinds of imagining that could be involved in our engagement with this work. We could imagine what it would be like to be the person who is doing the following. Or we could imagine what it would be like to be the person followed; but the problem here is that one has to imagine walking in ignorance of being followed, and this is no easy thing to do in the right way. We can also imagine ourselves in ignorance of being followed but 'from the outside', or from an external perspective. These issues are discussed in Peter Goldie's 'Dramatic irony and the external perspective', in *Narrative and Understanding Persons*. Edited by D. Hutto. Royal Institute of Philosophy Supplements Series, Cambridge: Cambridge University Press, 2007, 69–84.

82 We are indebted here to James Young's *Art and Knowledge*, London: Routledge, 2001. Young argues that conceptual art cannot yield knowledge. His arguments are complex, but we hope that in what follows we will have captured some of the essential features of his claims.

83 Oscar Wilde is supposed to have once said about drinking absinthe that, after drinking the first glass, you see things as you wish they were; after the second glass, you see them as you wish they were not; and after the third glass, you see things just as they are, and this is the most terrible

of all. One feels that Degas has painted things just as they are after the third glass.

84 For more on this, see Frank Jackson, 'Epiphenomenal Qualia', *Philosophical Quarterly* 32 (1982): 127–136 and 'What Mary Didn't Know', *Journal of Philosophy* 83(1986): 291–295.

85 For discussion of the virtues of art, see Dominic McIver Lopes' *Sight and Sensibility: Evaluating Pictures.* Oxford: Oxford University Press, 2005; Matthew Kieran's 'The Vice of Snobbery: Aesthetic Knowledge, Justification and Virtue in Art Appreciation', *Philosophical Quarterly* forthcoming, and Peter Goldie's and Dominic McIver Lopes' discussion of virtues of art in *The Aristotelian Society* Supplementary Volume 82, 2008, 179–211.

86 In his *Revealing Art*, London: Routledge, 2005, 126.

87 See, for example, *My Bed* (1998), http://www.saatchi-gallery.co.uk/artists/artpages/tracey_emin_my_bed.htm

88 This is at the heart of Young's complaint in his *Art and Knowledge* about discourse-dependent artworks, specifically about *avant garde* art.

89 In his *Eminent Victorians*, New York: Knickerbocker Press, 1918, 168.

90 For a precise and accessible account of what it is for a feature to be adaptive, see Ellen Dissanayake, *Homo Aestheticus*, Washington: University of Washington Press, 1995.

91 In his *The Philosophy of Art*, Oxford: Blackwell, 2006, 4. Davies' excellent book has a thorough discussion of these and other evolutionary accounts of art, including a helpful bibliography.

92 Some might object that such drives are not, in fact, part of our actual psychology, or at least that they cannot be proved to be. We will not address this objection, which rests on a thorough mistrust of psychoanalytic explanations in general. Richard Wollheim discusses such drives in his *Art and its Objects*, especially Section 45.

93 Anthony Savile, 'Imagination and Aesthetic Value', *British Journal of Aesthetics* 46 (2006): 248–258. The citation is from Kant's *Critique of Judgement*, Section 49.

94 Savile, 252. Savile relates these ideas of Kant to a more Freudian explanation, of the kind mentioned above.

95 Savile, in our view, tends to make *beauty* too central an aspect of our human need for art.

96 Richard Wollheim, 'Why is Drawing Interesting?', in *British Journal of Aesthetics* 45, (2005): 1–10.

97 In the preface to *The Nigger of The 'Narcissus'*. Edited by C. Watts. London: Penguin, 1897/1963, xlviii. For a more detailed discussion of Conrad

here, see Peter Goldie's '*La Grande Illusion* as a work of art', in *Ethics at the Cinema*. Edited by Ward Jones and Sam Vice. Oxford: Oxford University Press, 2009.

98 Kant, *Critique of Judgement*, Section 19.

99 Ibid. Section 40.

Index